Living Consciously

Living Consciously

COLLECTED ESSAYS

Jorge Waxemberg

Cafh Foundation, Inc.
New York, New York

*Copyright © 1996 by Cafh Foundation, Inc.
All rights reserved.*

*International Standard Book Number 0-9609102-2-0
Library of Congress Catalog Card Number 95-70003*

*Cafh Foundation, Inc.
2061 Broadway, New York, New York 10023*

Printed in the United States of America

CONTENTS

INTRODUCTION 1

PART ONE: *Understanding Relationships*

Common Ground 5
Points of View 9
Conviviality 14

Problems and Solutions 18
Universality 22

Our Relationship with Choice 28
Our Relationship with Personal Characteristics 35

PART TWO: *Developing Physical and Spiritual Health*

Physical Health 53
Two Facets of Well-Being 59

Alternatives 62
Dealing with Anger 67

Moving beyond Prejudices 74
Understanding Differences 80

PART THREE: *Discovering Our Vocation*

The Yearning for Meaning 87
Living Consciously 91

The Innermost Sanctum 98
Finding the Road 102

Mysticism in Our Lives 108

ABOUT CAFH 118

Introduction

We see today many publications on spiritual topics, and we hear from writers, philosophers, contemplatives, and religious thinkers from many traditions and ways of life. The quarterly journal *Seeds of Unfolding*, published by Cafh Foundation, has been a valuable vehicle for the ideas that are reshaping our changing world. Since the first issue appeared in 1982, we have been privileged to see many inspiring articles on spiritual topics by Jorge Waxemberg, the spiritual director of Cafh.

This book is a collection of his essays written over a twelve-year period, all of which originally appeared in *Seeds*. The articles range from such diverse (and yet, we will see, interrelated) subjects as developing physical health, living meaningful relationships, and unfolding the spiritual dimension of our lives. We find here essays that are simple and yet lead us to deep reflection, giving us ideas and material to put to use in our daily lives. For spiritual life, as we discover by reading on, is learning to live consciously.

It is our hope that this book will bring together an accessible and inspiring anthology of ideas for enriching our inner lives and working for the good of humanity.

Patricia Colleran
Carolyn Cooper
Kay Engelsmann
Jeri Prober
Don Witscher

March 1995

Understanding Relationships

Common Ground............ 5

Points of View.................. 9

Conviviality...................... 14

Problems and Solutions.. 18

Universality....................... 22

Our Relationship
with Choice....................... 28

Our Relationship with
Personal Characteristics.. 35

Common Ground

> *What we have in common constitutes a much more powerful bond than the differences we use against one another.*

In each of our daily activities we need a lot of effort and no small amount of skill to be able to behave as expected. At work, for example, we are supposed to carry out our obligations well and to conduct ourselves in such a way as is in keeping with our position. We have to treat clients in a certain way and supervisors in another. When we leave work and take the bus or train, we must act in one way; if we speak with a stranger, we express ourselves in yet a different manner.

We continuously change the way we express ourselves according to changing situations. We adapt so spontaneously and quickly that we think that we are always the same. We think we never change how we act and relate. One of the fundamental aspects of our education is precisely this: knowing how to behave in an appropriate way in all circumstances and recognizing the difference between one situation and another. Thanks to this capacity, it is possible for us to maintain a system of relationships which is very complex but, at the same time, is not burdensome nor that hard to maintain.

Even so, many of us are not satisfied with the way we relate, not because it is bad, but because it is superficial. We would like to establish deeper, more meaningful relationships. It is obvious that we cannot do this with everyone, but we wish we could with at least those we are close to. Unfortunately, this is something that we do not always find easy to do.

To achieve a good relationship within the framework of our daily activities, we need to exercise a great deal of control over ourselves. We have to absorb annoyances and difficulties without appearing frustrated. We have to maintain a certain demeanor at work and with associates. And because we cannot release our tension, it begins to build up. What better way to release it than when we meet a friend or arrive home?

Releasing our tension rarely opens up good communication with others. On the contrary, it is often a source of misunderstanding and mutual pain. Our friend also may want to unburden his problems on us, and at home others, too, tend to release their tensions and frustrations. We cannot hope to have a good relationship with someone if we cry on her shoulder or make her the recipient of our frustrations and reactions. Our friends and family may very well expect different behavior from us.

Common Ground

What can we do to improve the situation and transform it into a means of communicating more deeply with one another?

We can do a lot. We can begin by observing ourselves as we relate. We can see how we use others to release our frustrations or to get what we want. We can honestly look at the way we try to control others. As soon as we see ourselves a little more clearly, we realize that there are many little things we can start to do to improve our relationships.

Let's begin with a very simple fact about relationships: When we are with other people, we tend to emphasize our differences—contrasting opinions, customs, preferences, objectives. When this happens, we usually defend our position and others defend theirs. It is but a short step from this stage to an argument or serious misunderstanding. This approach, of emphasizing differences, seldom leads to good relationships or a real understanding between people. We need a different method.

Instead, we can attempt in any relationship we may have to uncover elements we share, what we could call "common ground." When we discover similarities, we find a common language, and through that common language a closer relationship begins, which can deepen with time and effort.

Differences are always relative to circumstances. Everyone undergoes different experiences. Our coworkers may be from different cultures and social conditions. Each personality is formed with its own characteristics. Even members of the same family are very different from each other. But we are all human beings, we are all sensitive to pain and joy, we all have difficulties, we all yearn for happiness, and we all seek the way to develop our possibilities.

Our human condition unites us. What we have in common constitutes a much more powerful bond than the differences we use against one another. In the end, what tends to separate us are elements of our own making which we ourselves can control and change. What unites us belongs to our human nature, to a history that is common to the whole human race and to the possibilities of all human beings. When we remain conscious of this common ground, and when our relationships unfold along this line, we automatically communicate better and find the channel by which we can understand one another deeply and permanently.

Points of View

The wider our horizons become, the wiser are our judgments and decisions.

How often it happens that well-intentioned persons have different opinions on the same subject: no matter how much they argue and discuss the issue, they cannot come to an agreement. Many times we have heard someone say, "It's impossible! No matter how I explain it, you still don't understand me!" We tend to think that it only takes an explanation of our opinions for everyone to see clearly that we are right. However, as we have all seen so often, this rarely works in relationships, between persons or between nations. Rather than trying to demonstrate the correctness of our opinions—which is what we usually do—we really should try to discover what our points of view are.

We must not confuse "opinion" with "point of view." Each point of view generates opinions. These opinions are coherent within the perspective of the particular point of view. All opinions can be correct if they are consistent with the point of view that produces them. For example, let's imagine a group of people who get together to plan a trip and can't agree on where to go. Some want to go to the mountains; others would rather go swimming in a river; still others prefer a walk in the woods. Since each person wants the group to take a trip to the best place, each has given an opinion according to the way he or she evaluates "places." But it is doubtful that they will arrive at an agreement, since at this level their opinions do not have anything in common. Everyone imagines that they agree because they all want to take a trip. But they don't really agree because each one understands the trip in his or her own way. If they realized that the problem is in the nature of their points of view, they might quickly come to understand one another. In this particular case, they could clarify the reason they are taking the trip in the first place. If the purpose is not to decide which place is best, but rather to go somewhere together, no one will hesitate to give up a preference for the sake of having a common objective.

Every time we have to evaluate or decide something, we cannot avoid taking a point of view. Sometimes we are aware of this, but more often we are not. It is better to choose a point of view consciously, considering all the options we have. In the majority of cases we can choose from a whole range of positions, from those which are strictly personal to those which are universal. For example, if I am a lawmaker, I can take any number of viewpoints: I can consider only my private interests; I can consider the interests of the group to which I belong; I can consider the interests of my nation or those of all humankind. In practice, this implies that, before giving an opinion or adopting a resolution, I have to ask myself which point of view I will base my decision on. Even though at times it seems that what we think and do does not have much relationship to anyone else, we all influence and are influenced by one another. The human race receives the consequences of the actions and decisions we each make. For this reason we must not forget others when we have to make decisions.

Undoubtedly, this way of thinking will force us to give up some of our preferences. We will move from a limited point of view to a more expansive one, and we will begin to see the whole of which each of us is only a little part.

The more we know, the broader is the vision with which we contemplate the world and life. Moreover, the wider our horizons become, the wiser are our judgments and decisions. When the legislator makes laws, he thinks of the needs and the well–being of his constituents. The better he knows history, the better he knows how to correct past errors. The better he knows the present, the better he knows how to prevent future ills.

Every time we have to make basic, far–reaching decisions, we must look at the whole, at the totality. Once a decision is made, we have to concentrate on the realization of the chosen objective.

The art of living consists in limiting oneself without losing vision; concentrating without ceasing to see the whole; viewing the whole without failing to give importance to details.

In certain cases it is necessary to begin from a reduced point of view to be able, eventually, to acquire a broader one. For example, I might be concerned with solving the world's problems. This is, of course, magnificent. But at the same time I need to limit my viewpoint and see whether in practice I am self-sufficient and really solve the problems I create for people around me. The good of the world must not be a daydream which prevents me from seeing what is actually within my power to improve in my daily life.

In other words, a broad point of view is made concrete by realizing reduced points of view. When a student sees how illness produces suffering, he can ask himself what he can do to alleviate it. While his global vision of human suffering allows him to understand that he cannot eliminate it totally, if he reduces his point of view he realizes that he can indeed help some people. He can decide, for example, to study very hard and become a surgeon. Of course, when he is later performing a delicate operation, he cannot have a cosmic vision of humanity; he has to concentrate completely on what he is doing at that moment. When he is working at his specialty, the surgeon reduces his point of view; when he leaves the hospital, his world expands.

Whenever we adopt an opinion or make a decision, we are choosing a point of view. If we

Points of View

are able to see that point of view clearly we can better foresee the consequences of our decisions and our way of thinking. Moreover, to see that particular point of view clearly often allows us to discover other points of view which, because they are broader, show us better possibilities.

Conviviality

The road of spiritual unfolding is a continuous process of deepening relationships.

Human beings live in relationship. We relate in some way or another with ourselves, with each other, with the world, with the entire universe. We live an organic, but unconscious, relationship with the earth. We establish conscious relationships with people. And, in the larger picture, we are an indissoluble and inseparable part of the universe.

But, for the most part, we do not recognize our relationships. Usually we are aware of only some of them, especially those that we establish voluntarily. Yet, in spite of what we recognize or understand, we live in relationship—with everyone and everything.

The road of spiritual unfolding is a continuous process of deepening relationships, simplifying and unifying the different ways we relate into a single, harmonious whole. It is likewise a process of transforming unconscious relationships into conscious ones.

When we think of relationships in this way, love has a new meaning. Love becomes the conscious, harmonious relationship we establish and develop with others. Divine Union, as the highest expression of love, is our conscious, harmonious relationship with everything—with the universe, with God.

Although our individual spiritual life is intimate and profound, it cannot be isolated from the life of the greater human community. The foundation of spiritual life is conviviality, and its unfolding depends on the deepening of relationships.

The soul unites with the Divine through souls, through all souls. One embraces the cosmos by including all its parts. One can pursue the infinite only by integrating the finite. Yet when we seek spiritual unfolding, many times we are not only unconscious of our relationships, but we also have little understanding of how to live well with others, even in the most elementary way.

Conviviality is an art that needs to be cultivated. Human beings have always dreamed of the perfect society and have imagined innumerable utopias. But no organizational change can produce a better society by itself unless we first learn how to live together in conscious, harmonious relationships.

Sometimes we overlook this fundamental understanding and aim to live a "spiritual" life. We then find ourselves living as though we were separate, as if my individual life was of sole importance in the universe. But spiritual unfolding is possible only when it is connected with the unfolding and deepening of the relationship that we have with everyone and everything.

The spiritual tradition that we inherit from all the great religions teaches us the first steps we need for a minimum degree of human relationship: not to kill, not to injure. That is, we must control ourselves enough so that we do not cause harm to others. The spiritual tradition also teaches the practice of virtues which help us to accept our neighbor: tolerance, patience, compassion. But we, as human beings, have not as yet really learned to live these teachings, even though these moral standards mark just the beginning of a basic human relationship. And once we do take these first steps, we still need to find a way to live a permanent and profound relationship with souls.

Spiritual unfolding demands continuous inner work, and this effort, to be effective, needs to be based on a method of perfecting relationships. When we are conscious of our relationships, we make every effort to remove any barriers we might place between ourselves and others. We work to master all our personal expressions— our gestures, for example, and our words and attitudes—and strive to prevent them from separating us from others. We look for that nexus that harmoniously links one person with another, each individual to the group, each group to the greater human society. Through self-control and our harmonious interaction

Conviviality

with others, we establish an indissoluble spiritual bond between ourselves and everyone.

We find, then, that for a spiritual life to be possible, it is not enough to meditate, to practice ascetic exercises for controlling the mind and the body. Our relationships need to be deepened; we work to make harmonious conviviality possible. Conviviality is the point of departure for reaching perfect integration—union with the Divine.

Our task, then, is to raise the level of our relationships. How will we do this? By recognizing a very simple fact: the more harmonious a relationship is, the less obvious it is. Think of the great harmonious relationships of the sun and the planets: they move in silent perfection, in complete union with one another. Likewise, when our relationships are harmonious, they pass unnoticed.

Destructive relationships, by contrast, are always obvious: anger, exaggerated gestures, physical confrontation, shouts, irony and insults leave no doubt that a relationship—an imperfect one, of course—is being established. A genuine, profound relationship is unobtrusive because no personal outbursts mar its harmony.

To live in conscious relationship is to live in harmonious participation, the perfection of conviviality.

Problems and Solutions

Only unfolding can give us the possibility of arriving at a more transcendent vision of our difficulties.

There can be no doubt that each person has the right to think for himself and to fulfill his ideals, but in practice we often deny this right to others. Obviously the level at which we confront our differences is not so developed as to allow us to live together in harmony and stimulate our unfolding as a human society.

When we come up against a problem, we try to solve it. But until now our solutions have not ended our problems. It is quite likely that we need to understand problems in a broader way rather than look for new solutions, since if a problem is not thoroughly understood, one does not have the basis for solving it.

The most serious problems we confront are neither natural catastrophes nor trials brought to us by destiny. They are the products of ourselves, of our way of living, working and relating. Therefore, our problems are principally the

Problems and Solutions

symptoms of our own failings. It is essential not to mistake symptoms for the problem itself.

When children play they often fight over toys, even when there are enough toys for everybody. If a more mature person does not intervene, their games could be reduced to tears, distress, and even hitting. Fighting, which is the way in which children war with each other, is the expression of their problem at the level of toys—in other words, at the level of the child. Each child imagines that the solution to his problem is to have all the toys to play with by himself. A mature person understands that that is not the solution, nor is it giving the children more toys—it is to teach them to relate in a way that permits them to grow as human beings: to live together, to share, and to participate.

In order to guide children we must be more mature than they are. As experienced adults, we understand the relationship between the child and his toys, and hence we know how to gradually orient the child in his process of unfolding.

As he matures, the child assigns a different value to his toys and discovers the value of aspects of life he has hitherto ignored. When the child grows up, he stops fighting over toys. He sometimes fights for other reasons, but only until he becomes inwardly mature and comes to understand his relationship to others from a broader and more elevated point of view.

The fact of becoming older and considering ourselves adults does not imply that we are mature in all aspects. In some respects we proceed as if we were children. We no longer fight over toys, but we do over other things: sometimes material things, sometimes over prestige, power, opinions.

Therefore, when we confront our problems we must remember that, in addition to the immediate solution, there is a broader one—that of working at another level, the level of inner unfolding.

Only unfolding can give us the possibility of arriving at a more transcendent vision of our difficulties. For example, when we consider the problem of hunger, we cannot avoid thinking that we must feed those who are hungry. But at the same time we know we cannot conceal the enormity of the problem of hunger with a few simple answers. There must be a terrible lack of maturity in our relationships as human beings for hunger to exist as a problem in this world. If we do not work inwardly, spiritually, to attain a better kind of relationship among human beings, our immediate solutions postpone or disguise our problems, but they do not resolve them.

To solve a problem, we need to begin by understanding it from our highest point of view. How do we do this? By maturing as human beings, by working on the process of spiritual unfolding, which all too often is interrupted before reaching its full development.

Each level of unfolding has its characteristic problems. The solution to these problems takes up a great deal of our daily work. But the work of

Problems and Solutions

our life is based on our capacity to progressively mature. Our own unfolding gradually changes the way we look at our problems. This change of the level of our vision of things eliminates the cause of our problems and allows us to attain a more harmonious, stable, and productive way of relating.

Universality

A universal point of view is not only the result of the work of specialized groups; it depends to a great degree on individual effort.

Every advance in knowledge demands a reevaluation of our interpretation of the world and life. Human knowledge is constantly evolving. Each day we know more; discoveries are made continuously, opening up new frontiers of knowledge. The history of humanity reveals not only the chronology of human events but also the process of the evolution of knowledge.

At first glance, this evolution does not seem to create conflicts but, in fact, it often does. Sometimes real revolutions result. Every step forward demands a change, for each discovery perfects the vision of everything believed to be known.

Some discoveries cause a restructuring of society. The invention of the printing press, and much later, telephone, television and computers, precipitated enormous changes, the effects of which we are still experiencing. Free access to

Universality

information and direct and instantaneous communication make the world smaller. Other discoveries oblige us to relocate ourselves within reality. Proof that the earth is neither flat nor the center of the universe, direct exploration of space, access to the world of the infinitesimally small—all this forces us to redefine our vision of the world and to reconsider our place in the cosmos. Every time we change the way we understand things for another, broader view, we also have to change the way we understand our surrounding reality, even the way we understand ourselves. For example, people of the Middle Ages had quite a different image of themselves and the world than the image we have of ourselves today.

In spite of the fact that we accept the idea that change is indispensable for progress, it is very difficult for us—not to say almost impossible—to recognize that the process of permanent change is a universal law and that it is, therefore, equally applicable to all areas of our lives, including our opinions and way of thinking. From the moment of birth on, we begin forming an idea of reality. Little by little we develop our opinions and vision of the world and life. While we are involved in this process we are eager to learn: we question, investigate and study. We absorb knowledge and each new piece of information enriches us and helps us to expand our understanding. When we reach the point where we feel sufficiently sure of what we know, we become less open and begin losing the capacity to change our interpretations. We are more inclined to defend our positions than to broaden them. It becomes more important to us to prove that we are right than to seek a truth which could show us that we are not.

This readiness to impose our own point of view gives rise to personal conflicts, but it doesn't stop there. History shows us the different visions people have had of the world and life, and how often one particular group of people tries to force its interpretation over another. Yet up until the present, the struggles have been between visions with the same limits to their idea of reality. If two groups argued over a philosophical concept, they both probably still agreed that the earth was flat. Today, the life span of one particular point of view is much briefer. Each day brings new advances in all fields of knowledge. It becomes necessary to adjust our vision to conditions that are evolving at a fast rate. In this process, the different concepts of reality held by successive generations may be observed with growing clarity. Since the rhythm of change is accelerating, we are now contemporary with several of those visions. Today the youngest generation is forming its own way of understanding things, since it has richer sources of information than previous generations had at the time their interpretations were crystallizing. There thus exist two kinds of confrontation: one between groups of the same generation with differing

Universality

opinions, and the other between generations that assign different limits to their realities.

What does all this mean for us today? Although we know that our way of seeing things is not perfect or final, many of us feel that "we are right," that our view is the most sensible, the most just, the best. It may be true that we tolerate different opinions and, ideally, give everyone the right to think and feel as he or she likes, but deep down we feel the need to justify our point of view by imagining that it is the broadest. We think it is universal and therefore the best for everyone. This attitude, which seems innocent at first, is possibly at the root of humankind's tragedies.

It is now time for us to learn the great lesson of history. In spite of the tremendous determination with which for centuries each human group has struggled to impose its vision of life, not one has ever reached that objective. No vision of the world, no doctrine, has been shared by all human beings.

Of course, this does not mean that a particular viewpoint is harmful or inferior. On the contrary, each has the possibility of being the best, within its limits. For example, my understanding of sickness may not be the most perfect. Nevertheless, it may be very useful to me if it helps me to cure myself. Moreover, if I accept that my understanding of sickness is imperfect, I am always alert to the new discoveries which might help me in the future. By remaining conscious of the limits of my knowledge, I have the opportunity to broaden it continuously. I do not become enclosed in my way of understanding. I desire to learn and improve what I already know. Therefore, although different schools of thought exist in all fields, as long as each recognizes the limitations of its point of view, every advance a particular school makes will be of benefit to the others, since all will be prepared to take advantage of it. In this way, everyone's work will be useful in generating a more universal vision of the world and life.

However, a universal point of view is not only the result of the work of specialized groups; it depends to a great degree on individual effort. If it does not happen in each of us, individually, it does not happen anywhere. Effort is fundamental. It allows us to develop our capacity to respond to a broader point of view than the one we have. Even if we are shown a more universal point of view, we deal with it in the same way we do with any information we receive—we limit or expand it according to the scope of our interpretation of life. For example, if we learn that outer space is habitable, we may consider space as a possible place to take a vacation, or as providing an opportunity to develop a society that will have a more harmonious relationship with the universe.

It is not easy to broaden our viewpoint. However, if we were able to change our attitude just a little, that path would be clearer. If we realized how limited our view is, we could apply the lesson history has taught us. We could also

Universality

place more emphasis on the need to examine and perfect our vision, instead of always struggling to impose it. From this standpoint, we are all in the same situation: we all need to broaden our point of view. This is a work that each person does within himself. It cannot be forced upon someone else. It is a victory that each person can achieve in his or her own heart. Perhaps this is the road we need to take toward a more harmonious and peaceful world.

Our Relationship with Choice

> *To unfold spiritually one must limit oneself voluntarily and consciously within a method of life.*

We are continuously making choices, some conscious, others unconscious, all of which form a kind of line, a trajectory of our lives. We need to realize the kind of trajectory we are tracing with our choices and the results they bring to ourselves and others.

We are not always aware of this trajectory. We might be more concerned with the success or failure of our endeavors. Actually, though, it is more important for us to understand the extent to which our choices determine the quality of our lives. The trajectory that we are tracing can be consciously changed through the wise use of our capacity to choose.

Every moment presents us with options, but we rarely make real choices. We may simply react to the situations before us. Or we might follow old habits or be affected by the mental currents of

Our Relationship with Choice

the time. Sometimes we think that we do not need to choose, and other times we think it does not matter what we choose. But in spite of what we might think, each choice, conscious or unconscious, has its effect on us and others.

There are times when we look at the choices we've made and we feel dissatisfied, unhappy with our lives and the stretch of road we see ahead of us. We imagine how we would like to live, what we would like to be, what we would like to achieve. Although dreaming about our possibilities may bring us sweet moments of illusion, we still have to face life, which is sometimes difficult, sad and seemingly impossible to change.

Instead of abandoning ourselves to a dream of what we would like to be and do—which moves us to reject what we are and what we do—we need to learn to discern the difference between the illusions created by the imagination and the real possibilities we have to choose from. In other words, we can establish a conscious and continuous relationship with choice which, we will discover, is the way to live our lives fully.

To be able to choose, we have to have a clear idea of what we want. If we were to ask several people what they wanted to attain in life, their answers probably could be summarized very simply: they would like to satisfy their desires, feel happy, be fulfilled. But each of us is different, and we define these longings differently. In our imaginations, we think of the companionship, the achievements and the success that this sense of fulfillment and happiness would bring. Meanwhile, most of the time, we truly dislike our present situation which, like any situation, implies limitations, difficulties and a certain amount of suffering.

This contradiction between what we want and what we actually have produces a continuous feeling of discomfort in us. What can I do? First, I can review my present situation and identify those things I cannot change. I cannot change, for example, my age, my experiences, those things I have done and not done during my life, or my real capabilities. Nor can I change my commitments, such as those to home and children. The only way to liberate myself from a commitment is to fulfill it—I cannot change that.

To accept what I cannot change is a matter of common sense, and it helps me to stop daydreaming about impossible fantasies and illusory escapes. It would not make sense, for example, to imagine that I don't have any obligations when it is obvious that I do. Nor is it realistic to imagine that I have a particular talent when it is apparent that I do not.

To accept what I am is simply to accept my past. That, in itself, cleanses my mind and heart of something that may seem like a limitation but which really is the foundation on which I can constructively move ahead. I have to learn to use what I cannot change. Knowing this enables me to determine what my options are, what are my real possibilities.

Then I am ready to choose.

How then do I choose well? Some people, facing the choices before them, ask: How can I choose if I am not sure? Shouldn't I try different things, investigate all options, until no doubt remains about what I want? Certainly it is helpful and necessary to investigate. But if we wait to make a decision until we are absolutely sure, until there is no doubt left, it is not likely that we will ever fulfill anything of value.

Our choices always imply an element of risk, a margin of uncertainty. Doubt is ever present in the human condition. Sometimes doubt is hidden in a corner of our minds and only surfaces at moments of great difficulty. Yet there remains only one thing that is certain in human life: we are going to die. It is this certainty that in fact generates all our insecurity, doubts and vacillations. "Doubts" are really an aspect of our certainty of death, a condition of our reality.

Sometimes we do not face a decision because we would rather play around with our imagined possibilities, with all the things we would like to do or have. But nothing is achieved if we don't make a clear choice, and then make the effort needed to fulfill it.

In life, there are two kinds of fundamental choices we make.

The first we could call exterior choice. It is the choice of how I am going to use my life: what I am going to do, how I am going to do it, how

I will support myself. Exterior choice implies career decisions, training, commitments to other people, lifestyle, and concrete accomplishments in work and human relationships.

But my real possibilities are much broader than those represented by my exterior choice. That is why, regardless of the success I might have in the realization of my objectives, I so often do not attain the happiness and fulfillment that I had hoped for. After all, nothing can prevent me from growing older, declining physically, and gradually having fewer exterior possibilities.

We usually think that career, family, work, or success will bring us the fulfillment we always wanted. But the moment comes when we realize that we are missing something, that there must be something else in life besides the exterior choices we have made. And there is—another kind of choice.

This new choice is no longer an exterior commitment, either to others or to some particular thing I want to do. This new choice (perhaps the most important one I ever make) requires a commitment to myself, to my inner life. I have to choose if I will commit myself to the development of my integral being, to giving spiritual meaning to my life.

We call this choice inner choice.

Our inner choice is fundamental, and it marks a decisive moment in the life of every human being. It often requires us to reevaluate all previous choices and sometimes change our lives completely. The inner choice is made only once in life, and it is permanent.

Even so, we can fulfill this choice only if we are continuously conscious of it. To make an outward effort is not enough; we must resolve to remain inwardly aware, conscious of our inner processes and our tendency to find shelter in pretexts and justifications—our tendency to avoid facing the contradiction between what we do and what we know we yearn to do.

It is not enough to study texts, to practice exercises or to talk about inner life. We need concrete means for working innerly, and we have to apply these resources wisely and perseveringly.

On the path of spiritual unfolding, we need a method of life, spiritual direction, and continuous effort.

Every means, every method, implies a limitation. To unfold spiritually one needs to limit oneself voluntarily and consciously within a method of life. Spiritual realization, like any other realization, is attained through responsible and conscious limitation within the method and path appropriate for each person and for the chosen objective.

Spiritual direction is likewise indispensable. We all need the help and guidance of those who have already traversed the path we have chosen.

And without persevering effort, no realization is possible. No matter how high one's aspirations are, these aspirations in themselves are no more than a dream until one makes them a reality through a conscious, permanent, responsible effort.

Throughout our lives, we are continuously making choices. We tend to think that only some of them are important, but that is not so. All of them determine the trajectory of our lives. Yet it is the inner choice that we each make which gives meaning to our lives. Knowing how to choose spiritually produces a clear relationship with all our other choices in life.

Our Relationship with Personal Characteristics

> *Instead of imagining that one can change, that one can be "another" person, we have to contemplate our real possibility, which is the possibility to unfold.*

We all have characteristics: some are inherent, others are acquired. Together they shape the way we are and the way we express ourselves. Because characteristics are individual and vary from person to person, we will refer to them as "personal characteristics."

Just as everyone has a body—which enables one to be identified physically—everyone has a set of characteristics which distinguish him or her as a person. These characteristics reveal a person's temperament, traits, and the way he expresses himself and conducts himself in life.

There is no such thing as a set of perfect characteristics, although there is a certain consensus among us on what might be considered desirable characteristics. Most of the time when we think about our own characteristics, we identify the ones we feel are bad and those we think are good, based on what we want to achieve with them. Moreover, we usually say that a person is good or bad depending on the way his personal characteristics affect his relationship with us or with other people. Yet this way of appraising personal characteristics often leads to contradictions.

It might be that someone thinks he has a very good characteristic while those around him do not think it is good at all. For example, someone might feel very satisfied with his compulsive personality because it allows him to get what he wants from others. But we can be sure that those around him do not feel happy with the way he treats them.

It might be that another person is a hard worker and thinks that this is her best characteristic. But her capacity for work might negatively affect her relationship with those who cannot keep up with her tempo. She might even be continually comparing herself to others and criticizing them for not being able to work as she does. Besides, that characteristic—which might be advantageous in her office or shop—could prevent her from appreciating other aspects of life, such as being with her family, enjoying nature, sharing time with friends.

We need to know our personal characteristics because they are the means through which we express the way we work, relate to others and develop. They are also frequently the cause of many of the problems that trouble us.

What, then, is our relationship with our characteristics?

Since not all of my characteristics are good, often I am not satisfied with myself. And since it is very difficult for me to change these characteristics or even control them, I might become discouraged and think that no matter how great an effort I make, I cannot free myself from the limitations that my characteristics impose on me.

However, it is possible for me to establish a productive relationship with my personal characteristics. To do this, the first thing I have to do is to stop identifying with them.

Just as I do not identify myself with my eyes or nose or hands, I need not identify with other characteristics I have which, like temperament and character, express the way I act and react but do not show more than superficial aspects of myself.

It is helpful to remember that our characteristics are tools that allow us to perform the work of living. In this way, the distinction is kept clear between what one is and what one's achievements, occupation and characteristics are.

When I maintain this distance between myself and my characteristics, I have the possibility of using them fully and, what is more important, the chance to improve them. But if I identify with my characteristics, I cannot get to know them well or work on them.

For example, if I am very emotional and identify with this characteristic of mine, I tend to think that my emotions really express my true feelings. In reality, these very emotions are what confuse and cloud my discernment. Since I identify with everything I feel, I cannot distinguish the extent to which I am a slave of my emotional states. On the other hand, if I am able to keep a distance from the way I react emotionally, I can discover a deeper source of feeling. I can work better with the energy of my emotions and I am more likely to achieve a more serene and harmonious inner state, which lies behind my emotional ups and downs. Moreover, as this distance allows me to recognize the influence of my emotional characteristics over the way I think and relate to others, I learn to apply my judgment more effectively, and I can establish a relationship with others at a more spiritual level.

Something else happens, too, when we identify with our characteristics: as we do not like some of them, we dream about being different, about changing. Unfortunately, this desire alone does not take us very far. It is beautiful to see the desire to change, to be better, in a person. But this yearning needs to be well channelled if it is to lead to a true realization.

Instead of imagining that one can change, that one can be "another" person (which is usually nothing but a way of reacting against some of our characteristics), we have to contemplate our real possibility, which is the possibility to unfold. In other words, instead of abandoning myself to the game of imagining how I would like to be, I have to dedicate myself to the concrete work of my own unfolding. Practically speaking, I have to begin by getting to know my characteristics and working with them.

Our relationship with personal characteristics, then, has to be one of knowledge and work.

First, I must know what my characteristics are and how they express themselves. I have to discover which are helpful and which have a harmful effect on my unfolding. Then I must begin a systematic work on them.

At first glance it seems not only easy to recognize one's characteristics, but one actually thinks one already knows what they are. It is true that we know some of them, but we do not usually recognize the ones that cause problems for us.

Let's continue with the example we gave before: a hard worker might think that he does not get along with his colleagues because they are lazy and he works much harder than they. But the real reason he has trouble relating is because of his intolerance. An intolerant person rarely recognizes the full extent of his narrow-mindedness. It is unlikely that such a person will improve his relationship with others—he will always be thinking that others are responsible for his problems of relationship. Only when he recognizes his intolerance will he have the possibility of unfolding.

If I am very emotional, it is possible that I will not recognize this characteristic, thinking instead that I am sensitive. Then when I see that a certain circumstance produces a wave of emotion in me but does not awaken the same response in those around me, I might think that they are insensitive. I might judge them in such a way that it hurts my relationship with them.

Or it could be, in another circumstance, that I think of myself as a very sympathetic, warm and friendly person, and I need a lot of attention and a show of affection from others. If they don't respond the way I expect them to, I might think they are being indifferent. Perhaps this is not the case at all. It could be that I really am not that warm and friendly, I am actually quite selfish. I think mainly in terms of how others treat me. This, of course, prevents me from having harmonious relationships with others, and since I do not identify my real characteristic, I can't improve it even if I want to.

I might like to think that I am very spiritual and for that reason I do not trouble myself over material matters. I might even think this is my best characteristic. In truth it could be that I am irresponsible, and I don't want to make the necessary effort to keep my affairs in order.

The characteristics with which we are the most identified are the hardest ones for us to see. They are also precisely the ones we need to recognize and work on.

How can I learn not to identify with my personal characteristics? There is only one way—to overcome my defensiveness. When I am shown characteristics that I am glad I have, I feel very encouraged. But if someone tells me that I have a certain characteristic I don't like, I refuse to admit it, I react, I feel mortified. I might even behave negatively toward the one who showed it to me. The tendency to be defensive is very strong in us, and it shows little spiritual maturity. If I do not transcend it, I cannot unfold my real possibilities. I should feel genuine gratitude when people or circumstances help me see my inner nature more clearly. I can then discover characteristics that until then I did not want to recognize in myself.

I cannot work spiritually if I deceive myself about my characteristics, especially the ones I have to improve. I remember a conversation I overheard once in which someone said to a person:

"It seems that you are a little defensive."

She immediately replied, "I? Defensive? How could that be?"

This anecdote might make us smile, but we could all ask ourselves how we would react and feel if someone said the same thing to us.

To recognize the characteristics I have is fundamental to my spiritual unfolding. This recognition is to be profound and not cause reactions in me, either positive or negative.

It is natural for us to be happy about the characteristics that help us and to be sad about the ones we cannot control. However, if we react, we cannot work on ourselves. We need to keep alert in order not to react, not to defend ourselves. We also need to avoid criticizing the characteristics of others, for this simply blinds us to our own.

All of us have characteristics that may harm us and also ones that harm others. The first thing we get to know about a person are his characteristics. At the same time, that person sees in us only our characteristics. It is very helpful to learn to see the soul behind the characteristics, the real person, and therefore relate on a level beyond the movement of attraction and rejection.

When we try to improve our relationship with others, we do not always know how to go about it. We often limit ourselves to demanding that others change the aspects in themselves that bother us. But when they ask the same thing of us, we think they do not understand us. It is very difficult to achieve a good relationship in this way.

Just as it is helpful if I do not identify with my characteristics, likewise it is very beneficial if I do not identify other people with their characteristics. A person might have some extraordinary qualities and yet some of her characteristics can still bother me. On the other hand, another person might really attract me with his personal characteristics and yet we might not share the same values or spiritual aspirations.

Our Relationship with Personal Characteristics

In adolescence it is common for us to be attracted by other people's characteristics. Later, as we mature, we find another way of discerning.

My relationship with the characteristics of others needs to be based on understanding and tolerance.

In most cases when I feel hurt by others it is because I do not know how to relate with them on a deeper level than that of personal characteristics. Let's take this example: the shortcomings of my own child bother me less than the same characteristics in my neighbor's child. This is because my relationship with my own child goes beyond his exterior characteristics.

To deepen our relationship with others, we need to spiritualize the level on which we relate. We begin by accepting each and every person with all his characteristics.

To accept a person does not mean that my relationship with him is based on my capacity to put up with him. This would show that the quality of my relationship is very reduced. My relationship improves when it is based on understanding and love.

To accept others is also to recognize that I myself hurt them often, usually without recognizing it and by overlooking the hints I receive when such a thing is happening.

When I accept a person, I accept her in her circumstances and with her history. I never know to what extent the events that happened in her life influence her relationship with me, or the affect her personal history has on our relationship.

Above all, I have to understand that I myself influence the relationship to a great extent, and that many of the characteristics that bother me about her are actually the result of the way that person responds to my own characteristics.

When I feel irritation in my relationship with others I have to uncover the origin of my reactions, for there is where I need to work to be able to unfold.

No matter how good a relationship may be, there are always some difficulties, some unpleasant moments. To understand this is to accept the fact that all relationships entail some degree of suffering. When I accept the measure of sorrow that is always present in life, it become easier for me not to demand anything from others. This allows my relationships to be more harmonious and spiritual.

Our relationship with personal characteristics can be established on different levels. These levels, in turn, determine the ways in which I work with these characteristics.

To keep it simple, let's consider three levels of relationship with personal characteristics.

The first is the level of education, not in the sense of instruction but of upbringing. At this level we develop the capacity to control ourselves exteriorly, and we form habits of conduct. Conduct gives the standards upon which every kind of relationship is developed, and it determines the objective characteristics of the relationship.

Education always consists in the acquisition of a measure of control over one's characteristics. This control keeps our characteristics from harming us or others. Moreover, that same control allows us to channel our characteristics through habits of collaboration, work and communication so that they promote harmonious living conditions and the unfolding of our possibilities.

The second level is the psychological one. One works inwardly to become conscious of one's characteristics.

How do we spontaneously develop our characteristics?

We tend to develop some characteristics more than others. Some of these characteristics favor our unfolding and the deepening of our relationships, while others present an obstacle to it.

Therefore, on the psychological level, besides working to become conscious of the way in which we manifest ourselves, we work to unfold beneficial characteristics and to create habits through which we can control the ones which are not beneficial. This inner work would result in a real expansion of our relationship with others.

To be able to relate on a level of education and personal control is a big conquest. Nevertheless our relationship would be limited if it were only on that level. Working at the psychological level helps us to understand ourselves and others, and it opens a channel so that the way we love may expand and become spiritual. But for this inner work to produce a real transformation in us, it must reach the spiritual level.

Our personal characteristics are the channels through which our energy flows. We say that a characteristic is good when it channels our energy in a way that will produce the result we desire, and that a characteristic is counterproductive when its result opposes the sought-after goal.

It is therefore necessary, when evaluating characteristics, to have a point of reference: where would we like these characteristics to lead us? If we do not have an ideal in life, all inner work lacks meaning.

Moreover, without that ideal we don't know how to channel the energy we repress when we control some of our characteristics. If we do not transmute it, that energy turns against us and against others.

When I control an undesirable impulse—anger, for example—that energy remains in me. If I do not channel it in a better way, it grows in me until I can no longer control it, and then it overflows unpredictably or harms me. In other words, if I discharge my energy I harm others; if I repress it I harm myself. What can I do? I can guide it, so that the strength of my impulses are transmuted into the expansion of my state of consciousness and in the way I relate and love.

All spiritual work is synthesized, in the end, in the wise use of one's energy. Spiritual realization never comes from nothing. It always consists of the fruit of the transmutation of energy.

On the spiritual level, we also work on the notion of being. That is, spiritual work consists in discovering who we really are by transcending our identification with our characteristics.

When we consider our characteristics we usually say, "This is the way I am," as if the situation were definitive. If I do not identify with my characteristics I understand that what I am is one thing, and the way I am is another—no more than one of the many possibilities that I have in which to manifest myself. I also understand that instead of wanting to change what I am, I have to discover who I am and I have to work on the way I manifest myself. When I understand this in myself, I also understand it in others.

When I establish a distance between myself and my characteristics, I transform them into instruments which I need—just as I need my body—to be able to express myself and unfold.

If I am not motivated by an ideal, it is very unlikely that I will persevere in my inner work. At one moment my enthusiasm will stimulate me to make an effort, but when my enthusiasm is exhausted I will have no reason to continue making an effort.

What I need to do is to clearly establish the kind of unfolding I am looking for: what is the objective of my life? This is the only foundation upon which I can base myself. The type of objective I choose also determines the level of my unfolding.

If what I am seeking is material well-being, it is possible that I do not need to work further than the level of education. If I also want my relationship with others to be more profound than the usual superficial interactions, I need to work on the psychological level as well.

If I yearn for real peace and happiness, I need to understand that this is attained only on the spiritual level. To work on this level it is necessary to be motivated by the spiritual ideal.

We all want peace and happiness. Who doesn't? But not all of us understand that having peace and happiness doesn't mean we will always be enjoying life and never suffering. Instead of visualizing happiness as the opposite pole to work and suffering, we need to discover how to find peace and happiness within this very life, for we cannot evade life as it is.

The models of realization we know, which include those human beings who have brought us the material advances we enjoy as well as those who have showed us the spiritual realization we could attain, demonstrate for us that these realizations are based on continuous effort and renouncement. These persons not only show us our ideal, but also the road to realize it.

We all want to attain to realization. This is good. But the way we desire it is not always good. Only when we accept the fact that peace and happiness are the fruit of renouncement and sacrifice, will we ever be able to understand how to advance in our unfolding.

These are all good: exercises, study, techniques, if they are well-applied. But they alone do not give us what we yearn for. Yes, we need to work on our habits, our relationships, our personal characteristics. But if we do not renounce to ourselves, all this effort does not help us to transcend the level of our daily set of problems. We change problems without ever reaching a definitive realization.

Our desire for transformation and realization must necessarily be based on renouncement to our habitual personality: that is, the set of characteristics, of mental and emotional habits, with which we identify and manifest ourselves. In that way we will find the peace and happiness we yearn for.

Developing Physical and Spiritual Health

Physical Health 53

Two Facets of
Well-Being 59

Alternatives 62

Dealing with Anger 67

Moving beyond
Prejudices 74

Understanding
Differences 80

Physical Health

> *We need to look at our life in an integral way and see the body as an inseparable part of what we are. Body and mind are a unity.*

So much has been written about physical health in recent years, in the popular press as well as in serious scientific journals, so why do we have one more article on the subject here? Simply by the fact that so much continues to be written on health shows us that it is an unresolved issue. We are all concerned about physical fitness, yet not all of us have a clear plan of action for putting the recommendations of scientific research into practice. It is not that we are lacking information. Where we usually fail is in integrating into our lifestyles and habits the information we already have.

We can do much to keep ourselves well physically—the right amount of physical activity and the appropriate nutrition produce remarkable results. Yet, how many of us have persevered in following any program of diet and exercise that we ourselves decided to follow? Not many. We rely on our will power to carry out our resolutions, without recognizing that exercises and programs alone are not enough to motivate us to change our way of living. We need to change the way we see ourselves.

The body is an inseparable part of what we are. Body and mind are a unity. Physical health is not an isolated topic, one more among many others. It is something inseparable from the rest of life. The way in which the mind influences the body is well known—a simple emotion quickens our pulse; states of stress make our blood pressure rise. In the same way, our bodily state has an influence on our mental state. When our physical energy is low, we tend to get depressed; if our appearance is not good, we feel badly about ourselves. The question we are asking, then, is this: How can we use our minds to keep our bodies in the best possible condition?

First of all, we should look at the kind of attention we give our body. We do not always treat it in the same way. When we feel well we do not pay much attention to it. On the other hand, when we are sick it is hard for us to think about anything else. These two extremes are not very helpful. To try to ignore the consequences of habits we know are harmful is like running with our eyes closed; to think only about the state of our health is to fall into an obsession. Just as we worry about our economic situation and make plans for our future needs, we might also plan our way of living so that we would not get illnesses we

Physical Health

could easily prevent—or at least greatly reduce the risk of having them.

Certain habits of eating, lack of physical exercise, misuse of alcohol and tobacco, exposure to specific toxic substances and radiation are associated with the development of degenerative illnesses such as cardiovascular disease, some cancers and bone disorders. We certainly do not like to think about this, since it makes us feel guilty for not improving our way of living. The thought of illness is sad; it evokes tragedies we might have to undergo. Besides, life already accosts us with so many worries that we would rather not look at problems before they come up. Who likes to worry about illness when one is well? For this reason we tend to act only when problems appear, that is to say, by reaction. We think about health only when we feel sick, just as we go on a diet only when we have gained too much weight.

Neither ignorance nor escapism frees us from sickness and suffering. We need to become conscious of our habits and the risks we run when we do not change those that are harmful to us.

Our health is related to our habits of life, which in turn depend on our mental habits, on our attitude. Our way of living, working and confronting problems, as well as our habits of eating, relaxing and resting, all depend on the attitude we have. The first thing we need to look at, then, is our attitude, since it establishes the way we live.

An intelligent attitude encourages us to change

habits as we learn about more healthful, beneficial ones, instead of changing our habits only after we become sick.

Habits are often unconscious automatic movements. If we frequently adjust our eyeglasses, for example, we are not aware each time we do it because we do it so spontaneously. If we want to stop doing it, we find that the impulse to follow it is so strong that sometimes we don't have time to impose our will to stop ourselves. Likewise, if we resolve not to eat sweets, which has become a habit with us, we often remember our resolution only after having eaten them. That is why when we resolve to break a certain habit once and for all, we rarely succeed.

Choosing good habits consciously is not enough to triumph over well-established unhealthful habits. If it all depended on our capacity for choosing, we would of course not have too much difficulty. Who does not always desire the best? But in order to succeed in our good resolutions, we need our minds as allies. We need to remain conscious of the consequences of our habits, to develop a plan of action to improve them and not to take this work as a sacrifice, but as an asset in our development.

Calling to mind the harmful effects of the habits we want to change and the beneficial effects of those we want to take root in us helps us a great deal in improving our health habits. We can make this act of remembering a frequent

Physical Health

practice, for it is a source of strength we should not underestimate.

Simply keeping the risk in mind helps us to avoid danger until we learn to protect ourselves automatically. A fear of falling does not cause us to stop walking. Rather, we learn to walk well so that a fall is improbable. To walk safely is a habit that protects us, without our having to make an effort of will to walk well. Repeated movements rapidly turn into habits and, departing from there, become automatic—an extra effort is not necessary to carry them out.

Nevertheless, before a new habit takes root, not satisfying an impulse creates a void that begs to be filled. What gives better results is to choose beforehand something better to do, and to do it every time the same impulse appears. If we always respond in the same way to the same stimulus, little by little we introduce a new habit which gradually replaces the old one. To the degree that a new habit takes root, the old habit loses strength. Healthful habits of life become so much more attractive the more we practice them, because their results are evident: our body feels better and our mind is more serene. And our self–concept improves, because we see that we can gain control over our lives. To develop the capacity for creating new habits is fundamental for mastering the art of living. We learn, by changing counterproductive habits for better ones, to live in a way that is in harmony with what we know and believe.

A new habit is like a stranger. In the beginning we don't know how to relate to it, but as we get to know it better it becomes familiar and pleasing. There are no difficult habits; we create the difficulties with our way of thinking. When we decide to change one habit for another, it often happens that the new habit does not seem very attractive. It is not the new habit that is hard for us—it is thinking that we are losing something. As long as we feel that to change one habit for another healthier one is a sacrifice, it is very improbable that we will be successful in changing our bad habits.

To be interested in spiritual matters without taking into account our bodies would be just as limiting as paying attention to the body without considering our spiritual nature. Material life is intimately connected with spiritual life. The capacity for becoming conscious of our habits—and changing when we see that it is best to do so—is a fundamental aspect of our development as human beings. It is good for us to pay attention to physical health not only to feel better physically, but also to get to know our habits and to acquire mastery over our lives.

Two Facets of Well-Being

> *When we are well, we use our energy to produce and create better living conditions and new possibilities. Sickness, on the other hand, teaches us that the body is only a temporary instrument; this opens up new spiritual horizons for us.*

Few subjects are as important as physical well-being and its counterparts: sickness and death. Life depends on health. If we are lucky enough to be healthy, we tend to live as if this were always going to be the case. Getting sick seems like a catastrophe. Of course, health depends on many factors, some of which are beyond our control. Heredity, physical constitution, diseases and birth defects establish conditions that we are as yet unable to change. Even so, we can have a positive influence over our health. The main thing is to be conscious of the relationship that exists between health and our way of living, thinking and feeling and to remember that we cannot separate health from sickness, or life from death.

Spiritual unfolding is possible in any state of health. When we are well, we use our energy to produce and create better living conditions and new possibilities. Sickness, on the other hand, teaches us that the body is only a temporary instrument; this opens up new spiritual horizons for us. Yet living in a way that threatens our good health is harmful not only to ourselves but also to others. Staying as healthy as possible is an aspect of the responsibility we have toward society. We must all face the cost of illness and the limitations it brings.

The best thing is to stay in good health for most of our lives. We can, as a matter of fact, do a lot to make this possible. When we enjoy good health we should remember that keeping it depends to a large extent on our way of life. Of course, no one wants to get sick, but often our lifestyle is the cause of our sicknesses. Health is not simply a gift. In most cases it is up to us whether we are going to stay healthy or not.

However, the emphasis on staying in good health should not make us forget that we cannot completely avoid sickness, debilitation and death. It would be foolish to close our eyes and not look at these fundamental aspects of life. In order to keep spiritually healthy, it is good to look not only at the aspects of life we call positive. We need to learn to live with the limitations, pains and problems that illnesses bring. As the adage says, we should accept what we cannot avoid. We might add that even in the most critical situations we can always find new possibilities for realization. To live means to grow, produce and fulfill objectives; it also means to die. And, although we still don't completely understand the meaning of death, knowing how to die is perhaps as important as knowing how to live. Can we really separate life from death? The best way to learn to die is to learn to live well.

It is natural for us to fear death. But it is possible to overcome this fear. When we are able to, our life attains a depth and fullness that we could not have achieved in any other way. We should not think that death is the negation of life; it should be thought of, rather, as its culmination. The idea of death is not opposed to the joy of life, the plenitude of fulfillment, the peace of the heart. On the contrary, the consideration of death leads us to value each thing; when this happens, our life becomes permeated with a transcendental meaning. Moreover, the thought of death helps us to understand human pain and to develop the compassion and love which teach us to assist those who need us.

Alternatives

> *If we were able to identify some element that is common to all our problems, we would have the concrete means with which to work on all of them at the same time.*

Even if our life seems to run smoothly, we all have to confront problems every day. Although we care very much for loved ones and they care for us, we sometimes become hurt in our relationships with them, or we hurt them without meaning to. We like our jobs, but there are moments in which we find them tiresome or dull. It is often a hard struggle to excel or even just to survive. Sometimes we feel lonely and sad. Other times we are troubled by the world situation and humanity's uncertain future. Although these problems do not prevent us from living, they often feel like obstacles that stand in the way of our happiness or the possibility of inner peace. What can we do?

We usually try to endure our problems in the simplest way: we put up with them, we are patient. Of course, this does not put an end to

Alternatives

them, and when our resistance reaches its limit, we react. We either want others to change, or the situation to change, or we want to run away.

When we want others to change, we complain about them, and we expect them to change in such a way that they will not cause us problems anymore. But other people are not always predisposed to listen to us, and if they are, they usually are not ready to change.

When we want circumstances to change, we think, "I can't take it anymore. I never want to see that person again," or "That's final. I'm going to quit my job," or "I'll apply for a transfer." This approach, however, is also rarely successful. We find ourselves face-to-face with similar situations and problems again.

So we might decide on something more extreme: we run away, we escape in distractions, not thinking about the things that worry us or frighten us. We say, "I'll move," or "I'll quit school," or "I just won't think about it anymore." None of these attitudes do much to alleviate our troubles. We find similar problems in new places and with new situations. We might like to dream of a life without problems, but even in our dreams such a life is hard to imagine.

If instead of trying to make our problems disappear, we learn to work on them, they just might stop seeming like problems to us.

We cannot eliminate in a single blow the infinite number of obstacles life sets up against us, nor can we overcome them by confronting them one by one. Even if that were possible, it would be an endless task. If we were able to identify some element that is common to all our problems, we would have the concrete means with which to work on all of them at the same time. This would be much simpler and more practical. So let's try to look at problems from a more objective point of view.

In each particular problem we can easily identify some elements. The first is "the obstacle." Each problem seems to present a barrier that separates us from what we want. For most of us, "the obstacle" is the most easily identified element within our problems. The second element, ever present, is less often recognized. It is ourselves, the ones who are hindered by and suffer because of that obstacle. Obstacles change—whether they be people, situations, work, etc. We, on the other hand, are always ourselves. So we find in ourselves the common element to all our problems.

Besides ourselves as one element and the problem–causing obstacle as the other, there is the relationship between ourselves and that obstacle. Considering our problems within a system of relationships shows us new possibilities that are worthwhile exploring.

Behind each problem there is always a relationship. The problem that seems like an obstacle to our attainment of tranquility or happiness actually reveals a relationship between ourselves and the "cause" of the problem, and this relationship is the area that needs work.

What types of problems do we have?

We can have personal problems, aspects of ourselves which we don't like and which, in spite of everything, we cannot change: our physique, our age, our temperament, some of our limitations.

We can have interpersonal problems: poor relationships with others; individuals we can't stand or who can't stand us; troubles at home, at work, at school; obstacles in our own self-set objectives.

We can have problems with the society in which we live: our social class, our race, our ideas, our way of life.

There can be aspects of life that we have not been able to accept: sickness, old age, death.

In the case of personal problems, the "problem" lies in the relationship we have with ourselves.

In the case of interpersonal problems, the "problem" lies in the relationship we have with others.

In the case of the problems we have with society or the world, the "problem" lies in our relationship with the environment in which we live.

In the case of problems with pain, sickness, old age or death, the "problem" lies in our relationship with life.

If we work on our system of relationships, obstacles stop being problems and become centers of work. By improving our system of relationships we can change each obstacle into an opportunity for personal unfoldment. For example, if my problem at work is that my boss is authoritarian, I have different alternatives. One is to react and create such a hostile situation that he forces me to quit my job. Another is to put up with his authoritarianism. A third alternative is to work on my relationship with my boss. I cannot make him change. But neither can I ignore the negative effects of his inflexibility. I can discover new ways of dealing with him and his way of dealing with me which do not alter my inner stability and which do not destroy the pathways of communication we need to keep open. Instead of making a problem out of the obstacle, I work on that obstacle by improving my relationship. Each problem is nothing but a symptom which tells me that a relationship can and must become better.

Conscious and systematic work on our system of relationships is revealing and fruitful. Besides giving us a broader vision of ourselves and our lives, it allows a perspective that makes us feel part of a reality which gives meaning to what we do and feel. Moreover, discovering the way to work on our system of relationships gives us a greater inner strength because we understand that we are not at the mercy of what happens. On the contrary, the way we influence and are influenced by the environment in which we live is largely in our own hands.

Dealing with Anger

To react with anger adds a greater problem to the one we already have, and this self-created problem is the one that does the most damage.

Who does not feel annoyed when something does not turn out as we planned? When our annoyance increases and persists, we say we are angry. None of us likes to be a victim of our anger, but if we let ourselves get carried away by anger we multiply our problems. Although there may be no one formula against anger, we can still learn to relate with it. This relationship allows us to get to know ourselves better, to acquire control over our reactions, and to relate with others in a positive way.

We can isolate two aspects in our discussion of anger: the effect anger produces in us and the people around us, and the relationship we establish with anger itself.

When we are angry we let ourselves become immersed in aggressive feelings. The torrent of inner emotions that whirls inside us focuses our attention on the source of our irritation. It becomes difficult to think about anything else.

Even if we do not physically assault the person who made us angry, we attack with violent thoughts and feelings which we do not usually have. Pouring out our anger in criticisms and bad manners tends to feed the fire of our anger and also creates resentment in our relationships with others. If we allow anger to grow it can reach the point of becoming rage. When that happens we are no longer fully conscious of what we say or do.

Even if we are able to control ourselves exteriorly, anger makes us suffer and we look for someone to blame for our deep annoyance. We justify our anger by thinking we are right and we keep on arguing to prove our point. We rarely ask ourselves if it makes sense to react in the way we do. On the contrary, we come to believe that our anger is necessary, a "holy wrath," the cure for evil. We think that by reacting with anger we are doing something good, such as clarifying a situation, revealing the truth, or punishing a culprit.

Yet when we are angry we do not act or think sensibly. We are tense and we may actually be physically and emotionally unbalanced. In most cases our anger worsens the situation. To react with anger adds a greater problem to the one we already have, and this self–created problem is the one that does the most damage. To be angry is a form of vengeance which turns against our own selves.

Moreover, anger undermines our spiritual foundation. It actually moves us to act in the same

Dealing with Anger

way as the person we are reacting against. The very attitudes, actions or reactions that made us angry in the first place are now fueled in ourselves by our own anger. We might not necessarily throw a fit or a temper tantrum, but we still demonstrate that we don't have mastery over ourselves. Any anger implies the loss of exterior control. For this reason many spiritual directors teach that anger and resentment can be thought of as leaps backward in unfoldment: they cause us to wipe out with a single stroke what, over a long period of time and with great effort, we thought we had realized.

Compare, for example, what we feel and yearn for in moments of spiritual elevation with what we think, say and do when we are angry. We are like two different people. Even the most ordinary encounter can produce these angry feelings: How often has it happened that a person says something that irritates us, and then she goes on her way without giving another thought to us or to what she said? Meanwhile, we remain so involved in the incident that we mentally attack this person for a long time; we keep up an inner dispute with someone who does not even suspect that we are angry. Without realizing it, we act in the same way that we criticize.

Anger also produces a kind of inner alienation. We not only react against those who irritate us, but, since we are upset, our way of expressing ourselves is aggressive and wounding to everyone around us. How frequently we discharge our reactions upon people who don't have anything to do with the cause of our anger! We are not aware of the wounds we produce in others with our reactions. When we regain our composure it is already too late. The network that sustains our relationships with others is very delicate. Each of our reactions profoundly affects it and can ultimately destroy it. By reacting with anger, even our relationships with those we love deteriorate, and a moment may arrive in which we find ourselves inwardly alienated.

If we are quick to anger, it is probable that little by little we will lose the capacity to relate with anyone. Who wants to keep a relationship with someone who has the habit of discharging his irritations? It is good to remember that all we do and say is irreversible. Even if we get over our irritations and apologize, try to patch things up and forget what has happened, nevertheless, what is said is said, what is done is done, and we cannot do anything about it. Wounds may heal but they always leave a scar. Once there has been anger, nothing can ever again be what it was.

Therefore, in order to control the effects of anger it is necessary to establish a relationship with anger itself. First, we place a distance between ourselves and what happens to us; second, we learn to recognize our weak points; and, third, we develop the capacity to choose the way we will react when faced with contradictions.

To learn how to keep a distance between ourselves and our anger, we can perform a little

Dealing with Anger

exercise: we try to see ourselves from the outside, as others see us. We make a mental image of how we look to others. Of course, in order to do this well, we first need to separate our reactions from the ways in which we justify them, to stop, for example, our eagerness to prove that we are right. If we set aside our reasons for the way we feel, we can then concentrate on working objectively on our anger. This is a way to give ourselves some distance from what is happening to us and, although we may not be able to control ourselves completely, we will be able to keep enough objectivity to better understand the total situation.

Although at first the distance we are able to make between ourselves and what happens to us is very small and lasts only a short time, it is the first step that allows us to contemplate the events of our lives with greater magnitude. It is hard, for example, to appreciate a work of art if we hold it close to our face. The same thing happens to us when we want to appraise a situation; in order to understand what happens we have to learn to observe ourselves from a distance. If, for example, we are able to keep ourselves from reacting to criticism, we can contemplate the situation in the same way a friend who is with us sees it: from a distance. We can understand his advice—not to turn the matter into a personal problem but discover in ourselves what makes us react. Although at first glance this exercise does not seem to be so difficult, for many people it is a real triumph to be able to do it; it actually implies a fundamental step in the development of relationships.

To the degree to which we gain objectivity, we discover our most vulnerable areas—those which need no more than a light touch to awaken a strong reaction. We all have "sore spots" which we are not always ready to acknowledge. To accept our weak points is a fundamental step toward understanding our reactions. For example, if we recognize that we do not like to be shown our shortcomings, instead of becoming offended when someone points out our mistakes, we learn to listen and learn from them. When we accept the fact that we react and we know why we react, then we are less inclined to justify our anger. It shows us how we are and how we can improve our way of relating with others.

But is it possible not to react at all when something does not happen as we want it to? Of course this is not what we are attempting to achieve. Every healthy organism reacts when it is stimulated. However we do believe that it is possible to recognize that we do not have to respond in an unconscious and aggressive way. We can choose responses that promote our equilibrium and unfolding.

Even if we become aware of our weak points and know why we are angry, this does not mean that difficult moments and unpleasant events will disappear. But to achieve a distance and to recognize our way of reacting gives us a solid base

Dealing with Anger

from which to choose the best way of responding. If we learn to control ourselves, we have options. To gain distance, to know our weak points and the effects the latter produce in us are part of the method; they give us effective mastery over the situation. This control allows us to discover options where before we only saw inevitability.

Anger is not a passion that necessarily has to dominate us, but an aspect of our personality to which we may give the form and orientation which is most advantageous in every moment. The simple fact of having options at our disposal gives us the opportunity to continuously improve our relationship with the different people and circumstances we encounter in life. To learn to direct our feelings, to transform our irritations and anger into healthier and more positive attitudes is a good way to smooth our path and to learn how to hurdle obstacles that otherwise tend to overwhelm us.

Moving beyond Prejudices

> *It is not easy for me to accept that I have preconceptions about what I am. The very idea seems incredible to me: How can I have prejudices about myself?*

During the course of my life I have formed a view of things, of others and myself. Since this view is so familiar, it seems to me to be the most logical and sensible one, as well as the only correct one. I recognize that my "prejudices" are the preconceived ideas I might have about other people—those who seem different from me, strange or odd. I do not realize that the attitude which gives rise to these fixed ideas about other people is the same one that creates prejudices in how I see myself and reality in general.

Just as my prejudices about other people hinder me from knowing them and having a harmonious relationship with them, prejudices also block my development and do not allow me to broaden my vision of life and the world. I have a prejudice whenever I mistake my opinion for the truth. I

Moving beyond Prejudices

easily notice other people's prejudices but find it painful to accept that I too have prejudices. I see prejudices in others all the time but am unpleasantly surprised when someone points out my prejudices to me. I am used to thinking that my opinions reflect the truth and not a position I have taken in favor of or against someone or something. In fact, I believe I have always made an effort to overcome my preferences so that I am able to maintain a view which is equable and just. However, though my mind tells me the world is diverse and that my way of being, feeling and thinking is only one among many, I cannot help reacting when I see persons who live and think differently from the way I do. It is almost as if I see in them a potential danger from which I must protect myself.

When I stop and think about the nature of prejudices, I find that I am not free of them, even though intellectually I accept the idea that all human beings deserve the same respect and have the freedom to choose their beliefs and lifestyles.

With regard to knowledge in general, my opinions are simply based on what I read, on conversations, on partial or sporadic experiences, on ideas which happen to be in vogue. I do not find it strange that, though my direct experiences are limited, my ideas are firm and solid. Perhaps this is because I feel I cannot live without the security of thinking that what I believe is just the way I believe it is—and so I imagine that what I believe, I in fact know. In short, I confuse my presumptions with knowledge, my opinions with sure judgments.

Certainly it would not be sensible to reject all judgment simply because the judgment can never be definitive, for I need a base in order to do something in life. But if I remain aware that my judgments are necessarily provisional, I can keep my mind open to new conceptions, I can learn continuously and keep my way of understanding and my opinions up to date. I see this process already going on around me—in the sciences, for example. It is remarkable to note how rapidly theories that were believed to be firmly established are continuously being displaced by new discoveries. In the social order, growing intercommunication and interdependence among peoples—their economies, their politics and even their ideologies—impels us to accept other cultures, other opinions, other traditions. A more exact knowledge gives a broader scope. As a consequence, antagonism changes to tolerance and tolerance leads to acceptance, harmony and integration.

If I wish to develop a capacity to learn continuously, I need to leave aside my prejudices about reality. If I want to unfold fully as a person, I have to transcend the prejudices I have about myself. It is not easy for me to accept that I have preconceptions about what I am. The very idea seems incredible to me: How can I have prejudices about myself? My most well-founded opinions are those which refer to my person—after all, who or what can I know better than myself? Nothing is closer to me nor more continuously with me than myself.

Incredible as it may seem, in fact, I do not know myself well. I do not have even the most simple knowledge of my way of being, reacting and expressing myself. I have proof of the limits of my self-knowledge regularly—for my family members, friends, doctors, teachers and acquaintances know me in a different way than the way I know myself. They know me in a way that is sometimes so different that I am convinced it doesn't correspond with what I really am—I think others don't understand me, that I am not the way they tell me I am. This is so much so that a good deal of the conflict in my relationships with others originates in the differences between the perceptions they have of me and those I have of myself. This increases my frustrations, making me feel misunderstood or unjustly treated.

My prejudices about what I can accomplish prevent me not only from seeing my shortcomings, but also from distinguishing my possibilities—perhaps the best ones. On how many occasions do my friends, parents, or teachers try to persuade me to do something but then I fail to carry it out because I imagine I cannot do it? They see possibilities in me that I do not see in myself. It is a matter of accepting that others can see in me what I do not know how to see or am not capable of recognizing.

What it all comes down to is the fact that the knowledge I have of myself is partial and incomplete. Yet it is on this very foundation that I build firm ideas about what I am. My strengths, my shortcomings, my limitations, my abilities, and my prejudices about what I am prevent me from seeing all my possibilities.

The same thing frequently happens when new people arrive in a place. The new arrivals are not better or more capable than those who are already there. The difference is that they see in that place possibilities that those who live there do not. They can carry out something new because they believe they can do it. This also often occurs when a person imagines doing something different and decides to embark on an endeavor that others think is crazy or absurd. Such is the story of the great discoverers, those adventurers who crossed oceans, discovered lands, flew in newly invented aircraft and imagined it was possible to go out into space. What was different about them? It was that their imaginations went beyond the prejudices that were normal in their time and place; they believed something was possible which, in everyone else's eyes, was not.

I often think that my limitations are exterior, that other persons, the environment and circumstances are the obstacles which bar my unfolding. This might be true to a certain extent, but I am sure I will never be able to know my real possibilities until I look beyond the line drawn by my prejudices concerning what I am and what I

Moving beyond Prejudices

can accomplish. This refers not only to my exterior accomplishments, such as the material things and the academic degrees I can acquire, but also to my spiritual life. Beyond what I believe I know about myself, beyond what others believe they know about me, there lies the inner space still unexplored by me. There lie the spiritual possibilities only I can discover inwardly, as long as I love spiritual freedom enough to transcend my own prejudices.

The yearning for spiritual liberation impels me to move wholeheartedly toward the Divine; thus, to the degree to which I unfold spiritually, I encounter the barriers which I myself placed—without realizing what I was doing—between my soul and the Divine. These limitations are fundamentally inner; they come from the way in which I see myself and interpret spiritual life, my unfolding and the realization I yearn to attain. To the degree to which I transcend these prejudices, my relationship with others unfolds, my vision of the world and of life expands as well as the way in which I understand myself. Above all, I deepen the way I understand both my spiritual life and my relationship with the Divine.

Understanding Differences

> *The capability of contemplating the earth as a whole helps us to understand that cultures are interdependent.... In order for a universal vision—one suited to all human beings—to evolve, each culture needs to consider not only its own interpretation of life, but also the interpretations of other cultures.*

Humankind is made up of various cultures and peoples, each of which has its own vision of life and a particular way of solving its problems and fulfilling its possibilities. In every age there has been a predominant culture. Often it has tried to conquer other cultures or impose its own way on other peoples, but without ever entirely achieving its objective. No matter how great their dominion, all cultures have had to tolerate the existence of conceptions of life and the world that are different from their own. This makes us realize that there has never been a single worldview appropriate for everyone, and also that the differences among various cultures pertain to the functions each performs in the whole of humankind.

This is not difficult to understand in general terms. Nevertheless, it is not easy for us to recognize the characteristics and limitations of the culture to which we belong, nor is it easy for us to discover the function of our own culture in its relationship with others. However, we can see clearly the function that we as individuals have within our culture, especially when our work consists of something concrete. If I have been trained as a biochemist, for example, and perform that job in a laboratory, I have no doubts about my function. It is also easy for me to recognize that other people with other jobs contribute in a different way to society. I chose to study and train for the job I have, and others choose differently. This example can be a kind of analogy for understanding different cultures.

The chance to choose proves to me that there is more than one option and that not all options are appropriate for me. This does not make me think that the functions I do not choose are bad or wrong, but, on the contrary, it shows me that diversity brings progress and benefits for everyone. Thus I can choose the most suitable function for myself and my capabilities and live in peace. I know that others depend on the way I carry out my particular function and I depend on others as well. We see that all our functions are interdependent and that for all of us to fulfill our functions, each one of us must fulfill our own. We can't get to our job on time if our bus driver doesn't get to his job on time. It is clear that all our functions intertwine and that all are necessary.

However, the functions of great human groups—peoples and cultures—are not so easy to recognize. We do not always have a broad enough perspective from which to observe them, especially if they are contemporary. A culture's time is different from an individual's time. A culture's influence, its importance, and its consequences are measured in centuries rather than years. That is why it is not easy for us as individuals to understand our own culture. It is even less easy to understand a different one, with customs and values that don't fit in with ours.

A person does not choose his culture and his people in the same way he chooses a profession and a place to live. One is born into a culture and molded by it. A person tends to be so identified with his own culture that he can experience what we call "culture shock" when coming into contact with customs, points of view and values that may strike him at first not only as different, but as crazy, ignorant, or wrong. In the past, when cultures were not as closely bound together as they are today, it was common for conquerors to bring back objects or even persons from other cultures as curiosities to be exhibited. It was also common for them to try to convert other peoples to their own beliefs and customs. The imperial

Understanding Differences

culture considered that others were ignorant, and part of the work of conquest was to see that subjugated peoples change their values and customs for those of the victors. In this way the other cultures would become "civilized."

Today we have a different view. Close contact among the various peoples of the world and the capability of contemplating the earth as a whole helps us to understand that cultures are interdependent. We also realize that if different visions of the world exist today, it is because none of them is integral. In order for a universal vision—one suited to all human beings—to evolve, each culture needs to consider not only its own interpretation of life, but also the interpretations of other cultures.

Just as we have awakened to an ecological consciousness at the level of nature, so too at the human level we are developing an ecological consciousness. Vegetable and animal species form a chain in which each link is unique and irreplaceable; likewise, each human being and each people with its culture are indispensable. We are beginning to apply the same degree of tolerance and understanding that we demand from each other within our own culture to our relationship with other cultures.

How can we accelerate this process of harmonization? We can begin by cultivating a broader way of looking at what is different. Certainly each people, each culture, has its way of seeing itself and fulfilling its possibilities. But instead of using these differences in order to oppose one another, why not recognize that each culture contributes something that enriches the whole? Why not recognize that it is by integrating the differences and not by eliminating them that we can reach a universal vision of ourselves?

One of our limitations is to assume unconsciously that we are normal, and to make an evaluation of the differences we perceive based on our own concept of normality. Instead of evaluating the differences according to our assessment of what is good and bad, we can learn to see ourselves as part of a single body. In our body it is precisely the differences that allow the various organs to fulfill their functions and keep the body harmonious and healthy.

If we develop a deep respect for what seems different to us, it will be easier for us to broaden our vision and understand the function of each individual, group, people and culture in the whole of humankind.

Discovering Our Vocation

The Yearning for Meaning...................... 87

Living Consciously.......... 91

The Innermost Sanctum............................ 98

Finding the Road.............102

Mysticism in Our Lives..........................108

ABOUT CAFH................118

The Yearning for Meaning

*Love is a companion
in a work done alone
in the intimacy of each person's heart,
mind and soul.*

There are moments in a lifetime when a person becomes consciously aware of the mystery of life.

Such moments may occur at any age: in the discovery of a friend's need for comfort and love and of one's desire and ability to assist; in the sudden realization that a lifetime of possibilities and choices lies ahead; in the desire to devote one's life to something greater than oneself—to science, to finding a cure for a disease. Such moments may occur when one has everything in life, or when one encounters the inescapable sorrows of existence. Such moments may occur when one has everything one needs yet feels a strange uneasiness, a feeling that says, "but there has to be more to life than job, home, friends, movies.... There must be something underneath to tie it all together."

These are the moments in which the search for meaning in life surfaces. Usually the search is phrased in questions: "Where am I headed? What am I going to do in life?" "What is the meaning of my life?" For most, the answer to these questions remains a mystery, but this does not preclude a search for an answer, and it does not mean that one cannot come closer to it, step–by–step. This search for meaning, this yearning toward the unknown, is the foundation of spiritual life.

Now that we have asked our questions, where do we get the answers? Where does a person begin to look for meaning in life? It begins in the last place one usually thinks of looking: within the heart, mind and soul of the questioner.

Most people are accustomed to asking others questions and receiving guidance from their answers. The questions may be fairly trivial such as, "Is it going to rain again on Sunday?" or more serious, such as, "Do you still love me even though I got really angry at you?" People are accustomed to seeking the advice of family members, friends, therapists and counselors about the direction of their professional and personal lives. Advertising helps answer unspoken questions about how to fill free time and where to spend the next vacation.

Questions, questions, questions. And the answers or elements to form answers usually come from outside. But the search for meaning involves a different type of question and calls for a different type of response.

The Yearning for Meaning

"Who am I? What is the meaning of my life?" When I ask this kind of question, only one person can respond. Only one person has the elements needed to undertake such a search. That person is the very same one who asked the question. The necessary elements for beginning the search lie within myself—my mind, emotions and body. In other words, all the elements one requires to embark upon a spiritual quest exist within the person at the very moment he or she asks the question about meaning.

Mind, emotions and body can be directed and become useful tools in the search for meaning. I can thus learn how to move from the surface of life—where society, circumstances, family or peer group may dictate my thoughts and actions—to thinking, acting and looking at myself from an inner point of view.

The spiritual search for meaning in life is not like a research project in which one is expected to digest reams of information and draw conclusions based upon facts presented and interpreted by others. The yearning for meaning involves research within my own life. Research into how my mind works, what stimulates it to think in certain ways, what automatic mental response mechanisms exist, what ways my mind can assist in my search for meaning. The same research needs to be done with my emotions and with my body. The questioner's life is the laboratory in which the answer is sought. This quest within my life gradually takes me to the center of my being, to the discovery of an inner spiritual world, an unknown world to me.

Guidance in the search for meaning is indispensable. If one is not to fall into subjectivity, the seeker needs the help of someone who has more experience in the path of meaning. Thus finding a good spiritual director is essential.

How does the search begin? It begins when a person sincerely asks, "What is the meaning of my life?" and resolves to spend his or her life in pursuit of the answer. The second step is to undertake a program of spiritual exercises that assist in the search. These may consist of spending moments of quiet and recollection during which one withdraws from normal daily activities and habitual ways of thinking and feeling for a few minutes. One uses this time to reflect upon particular aspects of one's life and upon the direction in which one wishes to proceed. Meditation becomes a very important exercise.

However, exercises alone do not lead a person toward an inner spiritual awareness. Without a love for the search itself and a love of the possibilities within that await discovery, the quest could become a personal one. To be purely spiritual, one needs love. Love nurtures inner life, fosters attention and care in the practice of spiritual exercises and helps one persevere in the search when the way ahead seems dark. Love is a companion in a work done alone in the intimacy of each person's heart, mind and soul.

Living Consciously: The Mastering of Our Future

The most fundamental choice a person makes is what to do with his or her life.

We all yearn to live fully, to express our deepest intention, because we know that this is what gives meaning to our lives. How can we do this? We must learn to live consciously—in other words, we must learn how to choose.

In spite of the fact that there are things we cannot change, we still do have the possibility to choose consciously. This capacity to choose, no matter how limited it may seem to us, is what makes possible the progress of a society and the unfolding of an individual.

Of course, there are aspects of life that we can't change, the past, for example. We cannot even change our own past, much less that of humankind, and we cannot change any of its consequences. The best we can do with the past is accept it, since only by accepting it can we understand our own history and, more importantly, the moment we are living now.

The future, however, seems to be a new and unknown arena. Although we can speculate about it to a certain extent, we can never be sure what will happen. Our area of work is the present. The only way of having some positive control over our future is through our wise decisions in the present. Let us examine that margin we all have for altering the course of events, our capacity for consciously changing the direction of our lives by learning how to choose.

The most fundamental choice a person makes is what to do with his or her life. This choice is made not only with regard to how to earn a living. There is a deeper choice than the choice of a profession—one that affects all our decisions. It is the choice of the level on which to live. That level implies how we will live, it determines the meaning we give to our efforts and our successes. This decision touches every part of our lives and shapes the rest of our choices.

The world one chooses to live in depends on the meaning one gives to one's life. A person who is only interested in himself chooses to be the center of the world. Since in practice this is not possible, he limits his life to the circle of his interests. The rest is only the scenery he can look at, if and when he feels like it. A person who chooses a larger circle has interests encompassing a broader area. Some people choose universal ideals which

Living Consciously

include all human beings. Moreover, when one chooses the meaning of one's life, one is also choosing the meaning and the scope of one's struggles and achievements.

Once a person's fundamental choice has been made, he enters another level of choice. He has to choose the steps he will take to fulfill his ideal. The person who chooses a profession decides how and where she will be trained. The artist decides how he will fit himself for his work. The technician decides the skill she wishes to acquire and how she will acquire it. These decisions are not less important because they are secondary. They show us to what point the person is willing to follow the course he has chosen.

Each choice has its consequences and is a limitation. The consequences of one's decisions are usually easy to foresee. The person who chooses a professional career knows beforehand that several years of her life will be committed to study or to specialized work. The artist doesn't choose just the road to fame; he knows very well the effort that choice of life will demand of him. He knows not only that his chances for triumph are slim, but also that very likely he will never triumph.

When someone chooses something, she also chooses everything that choice implies. If I decide to buy something expensive, I cannot complain that it costs too much. If I spend my money on luxuries, I cannot complain that I don't have enough to buy food. Yet not everyone accepts this obvious fact. The person who chooses a selfish life doesn't always understand the consequences of that choice and often complains about the very thing she has chosen. She doesn't want to recognize that someone who doesn't care about others cannot expect others to care about her. She chooses what she wants, but rejects what it implies. She resists accepting that life has pleasant and unpleasant aspects and that it is impossible to separate them.

When one wants to have a home, one is, at the same time, choosing sharing, tolerance and acceptance of responsibilities one hasn't had before. When one chooses to have children, one is also choosing to nurture and educate them. One cannot be happy about having a child and then reject the work of caring for him. One cannot have one thing without the other. If someone is able to keep only what he wants and to get rid of what he doesn't, he is forcing others to carry the burden that is really his. This is also a choice and has consequences he cannot evade, even if he doesn't like them.

Every time we choose, we limit ourselves. This is impossible to avoid. To choose is precisely that: to elect one option among several. Sometimes we don't want to choose in order not to limit ourselves. But if we don't choose, we don't fulfill our goal. To be able to fulfill something, we need to concentrate our efforts. Even though we might be able to fulfill several objectives at

Living Consciously

the same time, we would never be able to fulfill all the possibilities we have.

We can never stop limiting ourselves because we cannot avoid deciding—even when we have not intended to make a decision. Not to choose is to decide to wait, to let time go by. This means that we are limiting ourselves by not channeling our efforts into something determined, something we would like to fulfill. Among our various options we make that choice not to choose. To limit ourselves is counterproductive when it reduces our capacity to understand and participate. But when we limit ourselves voluntarily, it makes us conscious of what we are doing, conscious of the responsibilities we assume and the meaning of our efforts and achievements.

Each choice we make determines our future possibilities. A traveler in New York can choose to go to Paris or to Hawaii. If she chooses to go to Paris, she can make a stopover in London. If she chooses to go to Hawaii, she can make a stopover in Los Angeles. Each choice establishes a course of action, and within each course of action there are certain possibilities. It is important to know, each time we choose, what possibilities we have from then on, and which options we are giving up in order to fulfill our desires.

Every time a person completes a stage, he encounters new possibilities. While a student is in high school he appears to have many options, but in fact he has just two fundamental ones: to finish high school or not. While he is still in school he can think about all he will be able to do when he graduates, but it is only after he completes his studies that he has the real option of going to college. New possibilities appear after the conclusion of a stage.

If we make a habit of choosing consciously and are aware of the stage we are going through, we have greater strength to fulfill our objectives without wasting time. We know beforehand the path we will follow, the responsibilities we will assume, the work we will begin and the obstacles we will have to overcome. But when we don't choose consciously, we simply drift—perhaps into danger. A person wandering on a mountain in the dark may come to the edge of the cliff without realizing it. The best he can hope for is to escape with his life and reach safe ground. That is, to get back safely to his starting point. Conscious choices help us to avoid not only wasting time but also suffering unnecessarily.

In addition to the choice of our ideal and the means to fulfill it, there are the countless decisions we make, every moment of each day. What mood will we be in today? How will we relate to others? What tasks will we do and how will we perform them? Though we may not be aware of it, the sum of the small decisions marks the path we will follow throughout the day, just as the wake behind the boat indicates in what direction it is headed.

Living Consciously

Sometimes a person is surprised upon arriving at a particular place because it isn't the one he thought he had chosen. However, it really was the place he was choosing when he made all his little decisions, the ones that seemed unimportant and which he didn't associate with his ideal. Let's take the example of a father who almost never spends time with his son. Whenever he has the opportunity, he chooses something else, without seeing what he is doing: he goes out with his friends, watches television, or takes a well-deserved nap. As time goes by, the father-son relationship becomes increasingly distant. Finally the father realizes that his son is like a stranger to him. Although he had always wanted to have the best possible relationship with his son, the little decisions he made every day produced a very different and unexpected result.

Although one's ideal is chosen once and forever, it is fulfilled at every moment. When we understand this, we become more and more conscious of our choices until the time comes when we are aware of all the choices we make and their consequences. To live consciously, then, is to choose intentionally the way we live all the time—the moments of great decisions and those of small, apparently insignificant ones. As we establish the habit of choosing consciously, we become better able to fulfill the fundamental intention of our lives.

The Innermost Sanctum

> *In all spiritual paths, sincere seekers have always found the Divine within themselves. They have taught that the path of unfolding and spiritual realization is interior and individual.*

In ancient Egypt, only the priests were allowed to enter the inner sanctum. The profane (pro = before + fanun = temple) remained outside it. The monumental temples were the testimonies of the Divine upon earth, but they did not permit access to ordinary human beings. The priests were the mediators between heaven and earth; the crowds gathered outside in the great temple courtyards and galleries. A direct relationship with the Divine was not possible for anyone but consecrated souls.

Since then we have advanced a great deal—today the horizons which open before us seem almost limitless. But any horizon sets off what is beyond it. When we push aside our horizons we are moving forward and are reminded that beyond the horizon lies something we do not see—the unknown. The more we know, the more conscious

The Innermost Sanctum

we are of what we do not know, and this deepens our yearning for the Divine.

Today we can enter temples and witness sacred ceremonies, but this does not always make us feel we are in direct contact with the Divine. We still tend to identify the spiritual with the places we go to pray. Compared with temples and religious ceremonies, the other aspects of our lives seem commonplace, materialistic, not transcendent at all.

The transcendent always seems to lie beyond our possibilities. Even if we have the habit of raising our thoughts to the Divine, it is difficult for us to integrate our spiritual life into our everyday material life. In a way, we act like the ancient Egyptians—we separate the sacred places from the profane, the Divine from the human, the spiritual from the material. Since we normally have to contend with quite worldly situations and problems, we feel profane. When we look within ourselves we do not find highly elevated feelings. Our actions do not easily show the spiritual aspect of our lives. We are then inclined to think that the realm of the spiritual and the Divine is outside ourselves, that it is a state we have to discover some place. We search outside ourselves for the solution to the relationship between the Divine and the human: we seek the formula for salvation, the miraculous intercession, the magic touch that will open the doors to the transcendent. We have the idea that there must always be someone or something between the spiritual and the material, between God and the human being.

The persons who have dedicated their whole lives to divine realization seem extraordinary to us, alien to our condition as common, ordinary people. They seem to live in a different world from ours, without the problems and tragedies we have to confront. It never occurs to us to think that we ourselves could be saints or mystics. No matter how high our aspirations may be, we feel that the spiritual is in some inaccessible place, behind closed doors that only some High Priest can open and walk through.

This is not so. In all spiritual paths, sincere seekers have always found the Divine within themselves. They have taught that the path of unfolding and spiritual realization is interior and individual. They have also emphasized that this work must be done with a sense of responsibility, determination and perseverance.

It is in our hands to discover our inner temple and establish, in a direct and simple way, our relationship with the Divine. But how can we do this while we live our usual, common, ordinary lives in society? This is, in fact, the art of spiritual life—to transform common, ordinary acts into the means for awakening the transcendent in our lives.

Nothing in life lacks transcendence. Each act, each instant is unique, irreplaceable, and contains a teaching we need to discover and learn. We can all achieve mastery in this art of living, but it

The Innermost Sanctum

would be difficult to attain it without the help of those who have already walked the path and without committing ourselves to the realization of that objective.

It is indispensable to find the appropriate guide. Yet we have to understand that no matter how perfect the teaching we are given, it is reduced to mere words if we do not realize it in our lives. Although it is necessary to receive good spiritual assistance, it is not enough. To attain real individual unfolding demands, on our part, a sincere commitment to work on ourselves. Our spiritual unfolding depends basically on our effort to attain it. That is to say, on the one hand we need orientation and, on the other, we depend on our individual work to realize in ourselves the spiritual teaching we receive.

The spiritual path is simple and direct. It teaches us that we are to seek the Divine within ourselves and that our unfolding depends on our effort. Divine assistance shows us the path, but we have to walk it.

All of us have the responsibility to choose our spiritual path and follow it to the end. It is not enough to go to the temple; it is necessary to go into its innermost sanctum. This path is interior and is open to all human beings in all circumstances.

Finding the Road

> *Life is a process of continuous unfolding; difficulties and contradictions are signs that show us how to keep advancing in the discovery of life and of ourselves.*

There are times we feel dissatisfied, unhappy with ourselves. If we have achieved whatever we were looking for, it might seem that the end result isn't worth very much. If, on the other hand, we feel we have failed in our endeavors, we might not be able to see new possibilities before us, even though it is evident that we do have options. Our dissatisfaction comes from a basic, underlying idea we have, that we probably aren't fully conscious of. We believe that our formation as a person is finished. We believe that, since we are adults, we must have already become what we will always be. We then tend to live on the defensive, feeling that each moment is an examination of our maturity and our capacity for solving life's conflicts. It is a tragic game of bluff, pretending that we have all the cards in our hand, that we are complete, finished human beings. Since, in the bottom of

Finding the Road

our hearts we know this is not so, we feel anxiety and restlessness.

These moments of discouragement which we would so much like to avoid can, in fact, be very valuable if we take advantage of them for our spiritual unfolding.

By the time we reach adulthood we believe that the period of our preparation is over, that we are already formed, and that from here on we must live just as we are. The process of development is evident through childhood and adolescence; later it tends to be less evident. We assume we must be developed once we are past the stage of physical growth. And we used to think—before technology became so accelerated—that we end our academic preparation as soon as we leave high school or college. But just as we know today that we need to keep updating our knowledge and information, we must also understand the need to develop as human beings all our lives. This need becomes evident when we are surprised by conflicts we don't know how to avoid or how to solve without causing new problems. That is when it is important to detect those moments of conflict and transform them into instruments of change and unfolding, and to understand that reaching adulthood means we are ready to begin to work on a conscious and responsible self-formation.

Of course we are all learning continuously from our experiences and vicissitudes, but when that learning is not systematic and conscious it gives rise to great suffering. We live as if we were driving a vehicle without looking, as if we had no choice but to bump into something before we realize that we have to change our course. Obviously it is not in our hands to control all of life's variables. However, this is not a problem, nor does it prevent us from working consciously on ourselves; it is simply a basic condition of our existence that we cannot ignore or reject. Our life is a process of continuous unfolding; difficulties and contradictions are signs that show us how to keep advancing in the discovery of life and of ourselves.

Just as we choose a profession and immerse ourselves in learning more and more about it, we can also continuously learn how to live, how to expand our horizons, how to discover new possibilities for fulfillment.

If we accept that we are not already formed, but that we need to develop as individuals and, especially, if we become determined to carry this out, we commence a new stage in our lives marked by our spiritual vocation.

We say that we have a spiritual vocation when we not only choose to unfold in a conscious way but also take steps to orient our efforts toward a higher end. It is not enough to be conscious—after all, it is possible to act negatively in a conscious way, even to the point of committing a crime. The result of a conscious work depends on the orientation we choose: why we are working and what we are working for, and what is the ideal that moves us.

Finding the Road

We choose a higher ideal when we orient our lives toward an objective that transcends selfishness. No matter how elevated an idea may seem originally, selfishness can turn it into an objective that is restricted by our particular interests. When we choose a higher ideal and take the task of our unfolding into our own hands, our life stretches toward new horizons. This process permanently leads us to transcend what we believed were our limits: those which defined our being, our condition and our possibilities.

The work of inner unfolding is not something that we do in addition to other things. It is our way of life. And our inner basis is our honesty with ourselves, our faith in the nobility of our vocation and our permanent dedication to its fulfillment. It is not enough to aspire to an ideal at some moments. We cannot base our life on passing feelings. If we want to fulfill our aspiration we have to commit our life to it. In order to achieve a real spiritual unfolding, all our efforts should be guiding us toward that end.

Just as in childhood and adolescence we need orientation and instruction, we also need this in adult life. We need the support of our companions on the road and, especially, the guidance and counsel of those who began before we did and who have already walked the path we yearn to walk. We look to examples of great human beings, such as Gandhi. We usually call attention to his achievements as a leader, but it is his remarkable unfolding, which was taking place during the course of his whole life, that can help us in our own lives. It transformed him from an unknown subject of an imperial empire into a spiritual figure who inspired and guided multitudes. Even today, he continues to inspire many of us in our spiritual work. Yet Gandhi never felt he was a superman; he had the humility to recognize himself always as an ordinary person. Notwithstanding his political triumphs, his fame and popularity, he persevered in his inner search; he worked continuously on himself in what he called the "search for truth." This vocation of spiritual unfolding is what differentiates Gandhi from his fellow statesmen—and is what can make a difference in our own lives. It is encouraging to know that it is within our reach to unfold as human beings, to learn from ourselves, to recognize our inner possibilities and fulfill them, and to do this as a lifetime of work.

The moment we stop forming physically and finish our studies—that moment in which we consider ourselves adults—is the moment we could begin dedicating ourselves fully to our spiritual unfolding. Our bodies are formed and our intellectual preparation allows us to take a place within our culture. We are now ready to initiate a conscious process of unfolding that will accompany us our whole life. This implies a turning point in our vision of ourselves and our possibilities. We no longer have to defend our errors or justify them. We are not enclosed within that crystallized mold

Finding the Road

which is the already–formed person, that image we see ourselves forced to keep propping up. On the contrary, the possibility of unfolding spiritually gives us freedom to learn, to correct our steps, to confront our best possibilities without fear of failure or discouragement, without feeling impelled to triumph before we can know we are living fully.

Mysticism in Our Lives

> *Mysticism gives life both universal perspective and direction. It makes us aware of our destiny.*

When we refer to mysticism, we usually think of something that seems disconnected from our daily lives. We imagine mysticism as something far away, remote—the choice of certain privileged souls who are able to dedicate their lives to a spiritual ideal. We never imagine that we could be mystics. We think that the only possibility open for us is to fit the spiritual side of our lives in between our other, more–pressing obligations.

Yet, if we analyze more deeply the teaching of great mystics, such as Swedenborg, Sri Aurobindo or Simone Weil, we discover that they never considered themselves extraordinary or different from other human beings. Like us, they fulfilled their personal and social responsibilities.

We find out that mystics are not different kinds of people nor do they live privileged lives. They face the same conditions as we do: illnesses, disillusionments, setbacks, misunderstandings. When we read about their lives we discover that they experience doubts, inner darkness, discouragement and anguish, as well as love, compassion and joy. What is it that makes the mystic different?

What makes them different is the attitude with which they orient their lives, understand their difficulties and respond to problems and challenges, and their attitude expresses itself in the decisions of everyday life. Daily life and mysticism are actually not contradictory. In fact, it is quite the opposite: mysticism makes daily life a school of unfolding.

Mysticism gives our life both universal perspective and direction. It makes us aware of our destiny. Daily life thus provides a wealth of experience that forms the foundation of an effective work on our spiritual unfolding. Let's try to synthesize here this symbiosis between daily life and mysticism.

1. Dedicating one's life to a transcendent objective

The first thing that we find when we look at the lives of the mystics is that they orient their lives toward an objective that includes all of humanity. They know they are part of a greater whole, and they act in accordance with that understanding.

Mystical work consists in continuously expanding the perception of this whole and in participating harmoniously with it, beginning with one's family, neighborhood, country, until one includes all of humanity. The greater one's circle of participation, the more profound is one's mysticism.

This way of understanding one's own life radically changes the way in which one does everything. Just as one changes one's lifestyle when one marries and has a family, one also changes one's life when one's family expands and embraces all living beings.

Besides having a dimension in space by encompassing more area and a greater number of beings, participation also has a dimension in time: one assumes responsibility for the future.

Short-term objectives have to respond to ultimate objectives. The mystic understands that the happiness of today must be a step toward a better world and a greater happiness tomorrow. This is something very important. Without a mystical perspective, one finds trouble around every corner: the satisfaction of the moment is transformed into the cause of a future sorrow; the easy carelessness with which one consumes something today generates a shortage that oneself—and society as a whole—suffers tomorrow. The effort to achieve a personal triumph often implies a progressive and irreversible deterioration in one's relationships with loved ones. The personal success of the moment can lead to future suffering for others.

Mystics extend the term of their objectives to include not only the well-being of the human beings living today but future humanity as well. What is good for one is always what is good for all. Mysticism gives the mystic a sense of the eternal, and this consciousness helps one to overcome the temptation to live for today without responsibility for the future. The future is not only one's future but the future of all humanity.

Mysticism is a point of view which encompasses life as a whole, thereby enabling us to see to what extent the decisions we make today could generate conflicts and sorrow tomorrow, or open up new possibilities, both for ourselves and for others. When we look at the lives of the people around us, we can see that their present situation is in large part determined by the apparently inconsequential attitudes and decisions they had made previously. It may surprise us that their attitudes appeared to be unimportant. But how significant they were! This shows us how important every single thing that we do is. Even our thoughts and feelings have immeasurable consequences in our lives.

When the young and successful lawyer Gandhi suffered discrimination in South Africa, he did not take it as a personal affront but as a point of support for understanding the great drama of human suffering. He came to realize that many groups of human beings were suffering from prejudice. Rather than fighting for his own vindication and rights, he decided instead to dedicate the rest of his life to correcting an unjust situation. The decision he made in that moment not only changed his own life radically but changed the life of humanity.

From the mystical point of view, everything that we do, as well as the way we do it, must lead towards an ever–increasing understanding of oneself, the world and life. Everything we think and do must lead to a deeper and more far-reaching participation with the world that we know. Not only that, our participation must extend to a greater whole, a reality that is beyond our present understanding and comprehension, but which includes each one of us and the world that we perceive.

2. Placing personal experiences within the context of humanity

By orienting life towards an objective that encompasses all of humanity, the mystic develops the capacity to understand his or her individual life. Personal experience with illness, old age, death, as well as happiness and joy, are understood when one places them within the context of all human life. This enables one to accept fully the laws of life and gives one the necessary discernment and strength to transform for the better those aspects of life that can be improved. This is what the mystics do, and this is what each one of us can do in every moment. And it is imperative that we do so.

When we are happy we don't think about the meaning of our happiness. We simply enjoy being happy. But when something causes us pain, we despair. We ask, "Why me?" and we don't find meaning in our suffering. What we don't realize is that it is not possible to understand a particular event if we don't refer to the whole context in which it belongs. We have to see it within the greater picture.

Each change, including the positive ones, occurs within a context of effort and suffering. Think about it. It always happens that way. Therefore, those times in which we suffer also include a message. It is necessary to learn to accept suffering in order to understand life.

3. Establishing a direct relationship with the Divine

Those who long for a mystical life are fundamentally seeking union with God. The mystics demonstrate that the way to this realization is by deepening the meaning of faith.

The life of the mystic is based on faith, prayer, and the permanent inner work of learning how to love.

Mystical faith is the basis of all faith; it precedes belief in something particular. It is the inner certainty that our possibility of uniting with the divine principle is inherent to the human condition; it is the certainty that our life has a meaning which leads us to the fullness of consciousness.

Mystical faith is based on the awareness of self and on the intrinsic human need to deepen this consciousness. That is to say, faith is the inner certainty of our infinite possibilities and our freedom to fulfill them. This faith is the source which gives us the strength to face difficulties and to unfold our consciousness.

This faith is not limited to the mystic; it is a necessary characteristic of the human condition.

Above all, it is a gift which must be guarded and cultivated, purifying it of prejudices, complexes, and petty desires.

Faith leads us to prayer. To pray requires us to remember the immensity and the mystery of life and our place in it. The conscious acceptance of our own littleness is the key to penetrating into the realm of prayer, into the free and spontaneous relationship between the soul and the Divine.

To pray is, essentially, to open the soul to the Divine, to penetrate one's own heart in order to discover one's own voice, and to use it, without the help of intermediaries or supports.

Everyone can pray. Even more than that, we need to pray. Prayer expands us and deepens our understanding. To pray, therefore, does not consist only in saying prayers, but most importantly, in maintaining a vital relationship with the divine mystery through an open and expectant attitude.

Just as we don't need "time" to recognize the beauty of the late afternoon light, a mere moment allows us to take consciousness that we are passengers on the ship of time that takes us towards the Divine. The mystics call these moments of awareness "stopping." It is good to make a habit of periodically stopping oneself in this way throughout the day. These little moments of awareness greatly influence the unfolding of our notion of being. The mystics also recommend that we dedicate some moments every day to remembering the main objective of our life and how we are fulfilling it. Imagine how much time we spend every day in a hurry, chasing after goals that are not even fundamental. How much more important it is to make the time to stop, become conscious of how we live and where we could be directing our efforts.

4. Working on our way of thinking and feeling

We live, as we have already noted, in accordance with the way we think and feel. Naturally it follows that improving thoughts and feelings helps us to live better, to actually transform our lives positively and give them meaning.

Where do we begin? Where do the mystics begin? First, we have to attain some degree of self–control. With practice and effort, we discover that this control increases in the measure in which we practice it.

We are used to letting our thoughts and feelings carry us away. We think that this is the way it is—we rarely think that we could do something about it. Yet, when we have to, we do control our thoughts—when certain obligations make it necessary, we can concentrate, and we can choose what to think and how. If we make a systematic practice of this capacity in order to ennoble our thoughts and feelings, this inner work will be reflected in all areas of our lives.

The way to do this is simple: every time we find ourselves with a negative or selfish thought or feeling, we replace it with one which is more positive and generous. Thoughts and feelings are negative not only when they are depressing, but when they are aggressive, and they hurt ourselves as much as others. Thoughts and feelings are selfish when they are centered exclusively on our own interests. These types of thoughts and feelings restrict our perception and our consciousness. When we replace such thoughts with ones that are more expansive, we perceive more, we understand more and we are stronger and more resourceful in making decisions for ourselves and the world.

This is why mystics say that a person's spiritual transformation begins when he or she learns how to generate one good thought, then another and another, thereby cultivating the habit of thinking and feeling expansively.

In summary, the mystics teach us that all human beings participate in the same reality, that all are subject to the vicissitudes of life, illness, decline and death. All of us face the challenge of the same fundamental questions: Who am I? Where did I come from? Where am I going? The lives of the mystics teach us that mysticism is a possibility for everyone, that it begins when one sees the particular circumstances of one's life within the greater framework of all of life. From this point of view, one appraises one's situation, faces one's difficulties, makes decisions and realizes one's potential. By keeping the great panorama of life always present, one is not confused when making decisions and choosing objectives. To work on one's way of thinking and feeling enables one's inner voice to speak from the heart, and one relates to the Divine directly, supported only on faith, on the certainty of the fact that, by being a human being with consciousness, one has the possibility of understanding who one is and where one is going.

This is the secret of transforming common, ordinary life into a full, meaningful life. And this is something any one of us can realize right now, wherever we are.

About Cafh

"Cafh" is an ancient word referring to the soul's yearning to know God. Its meaning implies the whole spectrum of the soul's spiritual unfolding, from the effort the soul makes to attain to God to the divine grace she receives to assist her in that effort. Cafh as a spiritual path was founded in 1937 in Argentina by Don Santiago Bovisio and expanded to Brazil, Chile and many other countries in the Americas. Chapters of Cafh are found today in the United States, Canada, Australia, Spain, France, Italy and Israel.

Cafh is not a large institution. Rather it consists of small groups of individuals who meet regularly and who share a common yearning to discover the meaning of life, to integrate that meaning into all aspects of daily experience and relationships. Cafh gives its members the gifts of a method of life, spiritual exercises such as meditation, and the individual assistance of spiritual direction. There are no fees to participate in Cafh. Love for humanity, the yearning to transform oneself and the willingness to undertake the task are the only requirements for walking the road of Cafh.

Cafh Foundation is a nonprofit organization founded in the United States to foster the ideals of Cafh and work for the spiritual development and welfare of all human beings. Besides publishing books on spiritual themes, Cafh Foundation publishes a journal, *Seeds of Unfolding*, devoted to the art of living. Cafh Foundation also sponsors conferences, retreats, courses of study, lectures, and dialogues on all aspects of spiritual life throughout the United States, Canada, and Australia.

For further information regarding the activities of Cafh Foundation, contact the address nearest you:

Atlanta
402 Theresa Court, N.W.
Tucker, GA 30084
(770) 564–9298

Boston
60 Sharon Street
Medford, MA 02155
(617) 483-3048

Chicago
2627 Poplar Street
Evanston, IL 60201
(708) 866–6515

Columbus
7626 Perry Road
Delaware, OH 43015
(614) 548–6586

Los Angeles
475 Ladera Street
Monterey Park, CA 91754
(213) 264–7611
e-mail: DBFSJF @ aol.com

Miami
P.O. Box 653754
Miami, FL 33265
(305) 279–8604

New York City	2061 Broadway New York, NY 10023 (212) 724–4260
New York	51 Cedar Lane Ossining, NY 10562 (914) 762–8150 e-mail: 70475.1071 @ compuserv.com
San Francisco	P.O. Box 4665 Berkeley, CA 94704 (510) 620–0222
Santa Fe	121 Arroyo Hondo Vistas Santa Fe, NM 87505 (505) 820–1959
St. Louis	750 N. Forest Avenue St. Louis, MO 63119 (314) 469–1087
Washington, DC	P.O. Box 13291 Arlington, VA 22219 (703) 525–7974
Sydney, Australia	404–B Old Northern Road Glenhaven, NSW 2154 (02) 899–6997
Toronto, Canada	2254 Taylor's Orchard Mississauga, Ontario L5B 2T3 (905) 276–2016

For further information regarding Cafh activities in Israel, contact the following addresses:

Jerusalem P.O.B. 3558
Jerusalem, 91035
Tele: 02-765083

Tel Aviv P.O.B. 480
Givalam, 53100
Tele: 03-5716693

Haifa P.O.B. 7731
Haifa, 31077
Tele: 04-8255329